THE PAPER
ARCHITECT

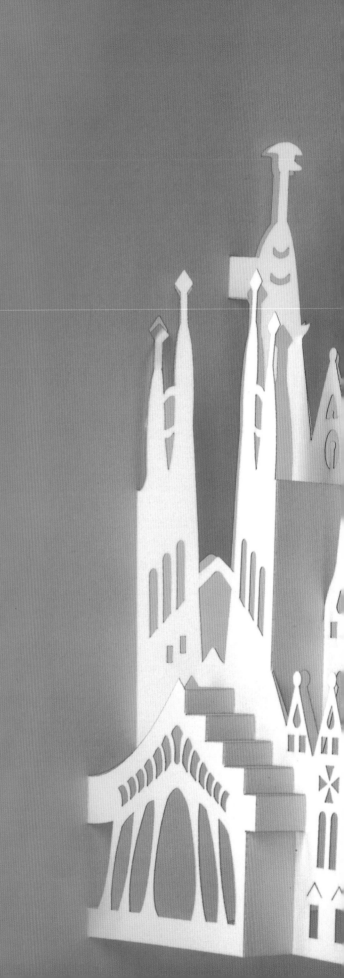

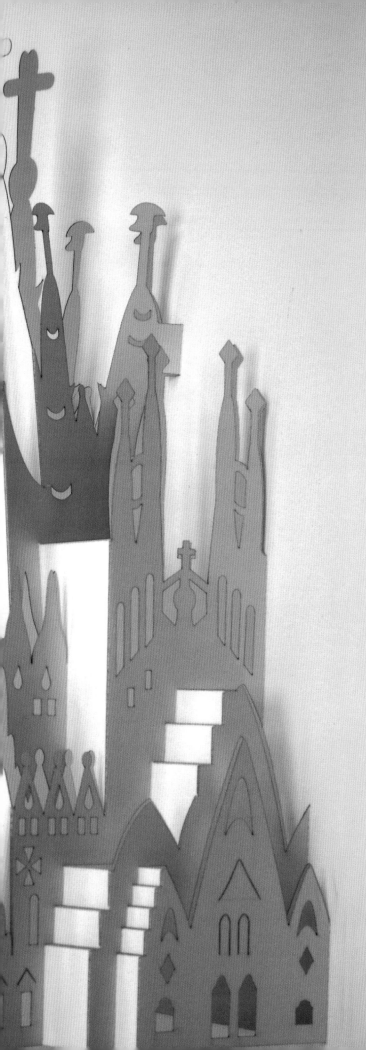

THE PAPER ARCHITECT

FOLD-IT-YOURSELF BUILDINGS AND STRUCTURES

With 20 Ready-to-Use Templates

María Victoria Garrido Bianchini

Ingrid Siliakus

Joyce Aysta

POTTER CRAFT

New York

Published in the United States by Potter Craft,
an imprint of the Crown Publishing Group,
a division of Random House, Inc., New York.
www.crownpublishing.com
www.pottercraft.com

POTTER CRAFT and colophon is a registered
trademark of Random House, Inc.

Published in Great Britain as *Architectural Origami*
by Apple Press Ltd, London.

Library of Congress Cataloging-in-Publication
Data is available upon request.
ISBN: 978-0-307-45147-7

Printed in China

This book was created by
Ivy Press
210 High Street, Lewes,
East Sussex, BN7 2NS, U.K.,
www.ivy-group.co.uk.

Creative Director **Peter Bridgewater**
Publisher **Jason Hook**
Editorial Director **Caroline Earle**
Art Director **Clare Harris**
Senior Project Editor **Dominique Page**
Designer **Glyn Bridgewater**
Illustrator **Kate Simunek**

10 9 8 7 6 5 4 3 2

First American Edition

Contents

 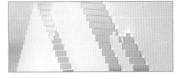

Introduction Getting Started

Folding combined with paper cutting to create paper buildings is known as *origami architecture*. Origami buildings can be startlingly realistic; when backlit, even the simplest become beautiful small replications—and they make wonderful little gifts or greetings cards. Although the craft has been around for many years, it has not been well documented. Today, it is growing rapidly in popularity, with enthusiasts all over the world sharing new designs on the Internet.

The twenty buildings featured in this book have been designed by three professional paper architects, but they have been rendered as simple to make as possible by the provision of templates at the back of the book. You can tear out a template to use directly, or copy (scan, photocopy, or trace) onto specialty cardstock for more variation.

The projects are organized according to their level of difficulty. It is best to start with the projects rated "Easy," and continue with these until you are confident with the basic techniques. It is also important to read the initial construction advice carefully before you begin (*see pages 8–9*). The success of your finished models depends largely on clean cutting and careful folding, so follow the advice given and do not be tempted to rush.

Set aside some clear time—an hour or two—for your first project. As with all origami, making these buildings can be an absorbing hobby; many paper architects find that the process of cutting and folding is in itself a calming, reflective activity. There is also a tremendous amount of creative satisfaction that comes from replicating a stunning piece of history.

What you need

You don't have to purchase expensive tools to make professional-looking origami: Only a clear work surface and a few items of equipment are required. The list below is a good starting point; all of the items are readily available from craft stores and websites (*see page 70 for suppliers*). The bone folder, which is a narrow tool for scoring paper, is not essential (although it is useful for marking folds), while a pair of tweezers can help you to make a good set of very short, sharp folds (for example, a flight of steps).

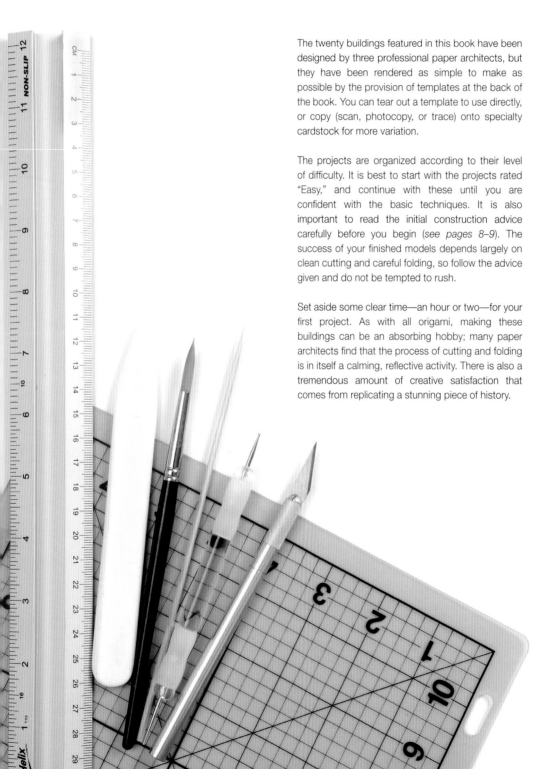

Tools and Materials

You will need

- Cutting mat (self-healing)

- Craft knife with #11 blades

- Metal ruler

- Needle-pointed stylus (a pen-shaped instrument for marking)

- Blunt knife

- Bamboo skewers and tweezers

- Removable tape or glue

Optional

- Bone folder

- Small paint brush (approx. 7"/18cm)

- Pencil with an eraser

- Scrap paper

- Cardstock of your choice

Copying and securing a template

You may, of course, wish to make the paper buildings more than once or change their appearance by using different cardstocks. To do this, you will need to copy your chosen template from the back of the book. You can scan, photocopy, or trace the image. **Please note, the template should be copied onto the back of your cardstock, so it does not show on the finished card.** If your cardstock is too heavy to feed through your printer or copy machine and you do not wish to trace it, you can copy it onto regular paper. Then, affix the template-copy to the back of your cardstock using the instructions provided to the right.

A note on suitable cardstock

Select a cardstock that measures 8½" x 11" (21 x 27.5cm) and make sure it is between 65# and 80# (160–250 g/sq m). Choose the weight according to your experience; the lighter the cardstock the easier it is to cut and fold.

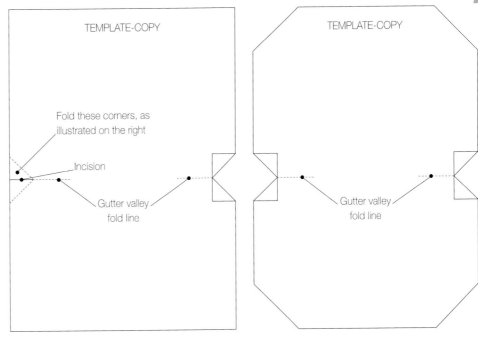

TEMPLATE-COPY

Fold these corners, as illustrated on the right

Incision

Gutter valley fold line

TEMPLATE-COPY

Gutter valley fold line

1 On your template-copy, make a small incision on the left and right of the gutter fold line with your craft knife. Now fold the corners of the incisions down, as shown. It then becomes easy to align the gutter fold line of the template with the gutter fold line of your cardstock.

2 Lightly mark the left and right of the gutter fold line in pencil on the back side of the cardstock. Cut off the corners of your template as shown. Place the template-copy over the reverse side of the cardstock. Secure the template-copy to the reverse side of the cardstock using removable tape on all four corners and on the folded-back incisions on the middle line. You are now ready to start cutting.

Basic Techniques Cutting and Folding

With your template on the cutting mat and your tools nearby, you are ready to start. You may be nervous cutting and folding your first card, but if you follow these guidelines you will quickly learn the craft. Remember that these templates are designed to fold in the correct direction; they are much stronger than they appear.

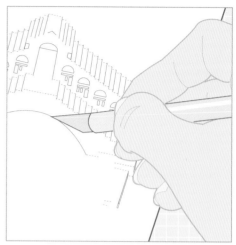

Cutting and scoring the design

When starting a template, it is advisable to use a new blade in your craft knife; it may seem an extravagance but a new blade makes it much easier to cut the lines in a single smooth action. Plus, a sharp-pointed blade is less likely to slip. If you have made a copy of the template, you will be cutting through two pieces of paper simultaneously, making a new blade especially important. Either way, make sure you always work on a cutting mat and use a metal ruler for a solid edge.

Always begin with the inside cutting lines—these are shown on the templates as dark blue solid lines (*see the illustration on the left*). Start with the smallest elements and the shortest lines. To cut circles or long curves, keep your blade pressed to the paper and turn the sheet with your other hand for a smoother line. It may be easier to work on all horizontal lines first before starting the verticals, to minimize the number of times that you need to turn the design. You will quickly discover which method suits you best.

Once the inside cutting lines are complete, move on to the outside cutting lines. Use the same methods as described above.

Template key

—————— **Cutting line** Solid lines; ones that are to be cut

·········· **Gutter fold** Dark blue dotted lines—the fold at the center of the card is always a valley fold

- - - - - **Valley fold** Light blue dashed lines that fold inward

· · · · · · **Mountain fold** Red dotted lines that fold outward

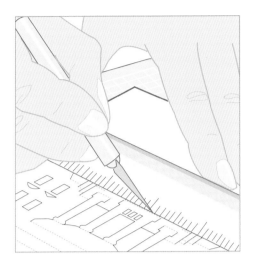

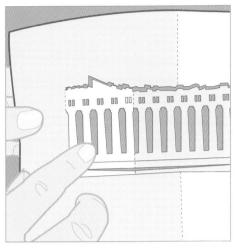

Half-cutting valley and mountain fold lines

Valley (inward) folds are always half-cut on the reverse side of the cardstock; mountain (outward) folds on the front. Use a ruler for all but the very short cuts. Before starting a template, practice on a spare sheet of identical cardstock until you achieve a sharp, easy-to-fold line, strong enough to be folded many times.

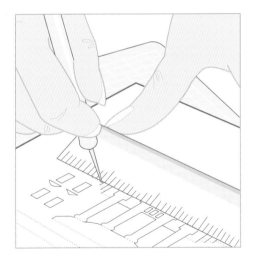

Once you are confident at half-cutting you can start on your chosen template. With your pattern printed (or template-copy secured) on the back of your card, mark all the mountain folds (red dotted lines) by making a hole with a stylus at each end of the line. Turn your cardstock to the front side and half-cut the mountain folds, locating the folds from the holes you made with the stylus.

Now turn your card to the reverse side and half-cut the valley folds (blue dashed lines) of the card. (If you are using a template-copy, mark the valley fold with a stylus just as you did for the mountain folds. Then remove the template-copy and half-cut the valley folds.) Your card is now ready to be folded.

Folding tips

Beginners are often concerned that they are going to tear or damage the cards. There's no need to be worried; these cards are designed to fold. All you are required to do is give them a little guidance. If you keep the following principles in your mind, it will help you to understand how the design works and enable you to master the folding process:

Each card is, in essence, a fancy accordion fold; for every mountain fold, there must be a valley fold. The folds create a series of 3-D rectangles. In each rectangle, the front wall must be as tall as the back wall and the roof must be as deep as the floor. You simply use your hands to encourage the folds in the direction you want them to go.

Folding a card works best if you keep one hand at the back and the other on the front of your cardstock. That way you can push and press the folds with both hands. Be gentle and fold the lines a little at a time. You don't need to crease the folds sharply, just give them an indication as to which direction they should move.

Always start by folding the gutter line inward as much as you can without risking damage to the other parts of the card. Keep returning to this point during the process to ensure the gutter is keeping its form.

If you find any fold lines tricky to reach, a good tip is to insert a long bamboo skewer behind the line to bring it toward you.

While folding a particular area, you may see another area start to fold itself inward or outward. Focus on this area next, and try to fold it a little further before moving on to any other area that starts to fold of its own accord.

When all the folds know their directions, place the card on a flat surface, and slowly press the card closed. You will feel all the folds collapse on themselves. If the card doesn't "feel right" when you try to close it, chances are that one or more of the folds are going in the wrong direction. Open the card and look at the folds. You should be able to see which folds are wrong and be able to reverse them.

Once the card is completely closed, use your thumbnail to crease the gutter fold. The pressure of your hand closing the card will have already sufficiently creased all of the interior folds.

Dos and Don'ts

- For all but Ingrid's designs, avoid pinching a fold with the thumb and forefinger of the same hand. It will be your first impulse, but it will not produce the right result.

- Where you find that some folds seem to form groups and all fold together, use that to your advantage. Sometimes you can use one fold as a lever to force the next fold to bend, and sometimes you can gather up several folds together (usually a staircase).

- Proceed slowly and gently, and work alternately from bottom to middle and from top to middle; by doing this, you will begin to see the design take shape.

Golden Gate Bridge **The Model**

Origami Architect Joyce Aysta

Difficulty Level Easy

Creating a paper version of this iconic structure gives you a sense of both the advanced engineering and the beauty of the Golden Gate Bridge. In fact, the model is a triumph in itself. The majority of the work for this design is in the cutting because the cables are so thin but once you get to the folding it is the easiest of all the models (*see template on page 71*).

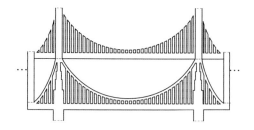

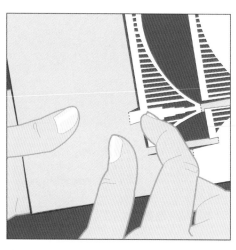

1 With the printed side facing you, hold the base of the template in one hand. Use your other hand to gently push the entire bridge outward.

2 Turn the template 180 degrees, and work the different components of the bridge. Since the valley folds were scored from the back, they should bend easily.

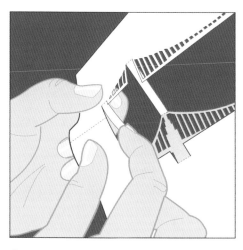

3 When pushing out the portals of the bridge, be particularly careful with the suspension cables—these are fairly fragile.

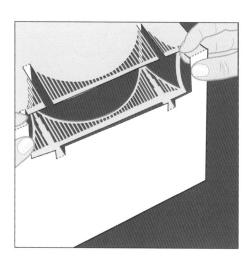

4 While holding the template on either side of the bridge, now crease the gutter fold.

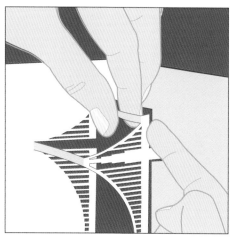

5 Turn over the template so that you are looking at the unprinted side. With one hand, hold the bridge by its joining end. Push with the index finger of your other hand to make the fold where the deck of the bridge would meet land on either side.

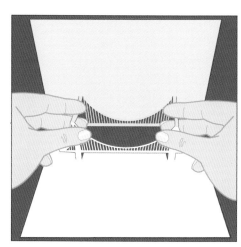

6 Lastly, crease the mountain folds at the top of the portals, then begin to close the card—the mountain folds will naturally follow. When you are sure that all the folds are correct, place the closed card on a flat surface and press down firmly. Open up to display your model.

Golden Gate Bridge Built *1933–1937* CE

Chief engineer **Joseph Baerman Strauss**
Senior engineer and designer **Charles Alton Ellis**
Consulting architect **Irving Morrow**

 Location San Francisco, U.S.A.

 Style Art Deco, Modernist

 Purpose Road bridge and footbridge

 Materials Reinforced concrete and steel

 Area (Including approaches) 808, 290 sq ft (73,899 sq m)

 Decoration Lead paint, acrylic paint

 Cost to build $27 million

 **Weight** 887,000 tons (804,673 tonnes)

The graceful Golden Gate Bridge spans the strait at the mouth of San Franciso Bay, connecting the city of San Francisco with Marin County to the north. Engineers were invited to submit proposals for a bridge in 1916, and eventually engineer Joseph Strauss (1870–1938) was chosen by the city on condition that he worked with consulting experts.

Even for a highly qualified team, the challenges faced were enormous. The bridge had to withstand earthquakes and Pacific gales—in the event of a 100-mph (160-km/h) wind, the deck had to be able to swing by as much as 27 feet (8.2m). Suspension bridges were not new when the bridge opened in 1937, ahead of schedule and under budget, but the Golden Gate featured the longest span, the longest, thickest cables, the tallest towers, and the largest anchorages of any suspension bridge built up to that time.

Construction began in early 1933, when workers built the steel-reinforced concrete anchorages to secure the bridge's cables at each end. The north pier (Marin County side) was then completed on a bedrock ledge 20 feet (6m) below water; in 1934, its north tower was added. It was followed by the south pier on the city side, which had to be built 100 feet (30.5m) high and in deeper water. Only after both sides were complete could the catwalk from tower to tower be installed, which was the first step toward laying the massive cables. These were attached to deep anchorages underground at either side, and were "spun" on site by laying more than 20,000 pencil-thin wires over the piers and weaving them together into their current thickness.

The finished Golden Gate Bridge has a number of Art Deco features, including the rectangular tower portals that decrease with height, the vertical ribbing on the horizontal tower bracings, the simplified pedestrian railings, and the lean, angled streetlights. The distinctive color was chosen by the consulting architect Irving Morrow. It is intended to blend in with the landscape but to stand out in fog—a weather phenomenon for which San Francisco is renowned.

Number of vehicles per year
Number of years to build
Height of the structure

= 5 million   T = 1 year

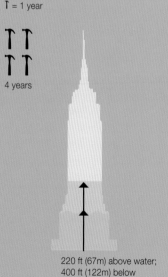

4 years

40 million vehicles

220 ft (67m) above water; 400 ft (122m) below

The bridge's two towers stand 746 feet (229m) tall—and are 500 feet (154m) above the roadway. The thick, steel towers are designed to deflect any stress that travels up the suspension cables from the roadway below during strong winds.

Pyramids of Giza Built *approx. 2580–2560* BCE
Architects **Unknown**

The three pyramids in Giza, Egypt, were commissioned by the pharaohs Khufu, Khafre, and Menkaure as burial chambers and paths to their after lives. Each pyramid has an adjoining mortuary temple, which was used for rituals to honor the dead kings. The three pyramids sit on the West Bank of the Nile, outside Cairo, in a 13-acre (5-ha) complex that also includes the famous Great Sphinx (a 200-foot (60-m) sandstone lion with a human head) which faces the rising sun.

Khufu built the largest of the pyramids, the Great Pyramid. It is the only one of the Seven Wonders of the ancient world still in existence. For nearly four thousand years it was the tallest man-made structure in the world, its sides rising at nearly 52 degrees up to 455 feet (138m), almost perfectly aligned to the cardinal points of the compass. The construction itself is a topic of speculation, but it probably involved a scaffolding ramp, along which the limestone blocks were rolled on logs and then levered up using wooden poles.

The original entrance of the Great Pyramid is on the north side, 55 feet (16.7m) above the base. A descending passage leads from there to a subterranean chamber. There is also an ascending passage which leads to a junction. From there, one corridor leads to the Queen's Chamber and another to the Grand Gallery. This in turn leads to the King's Chamber, constructed in granite.

The King's and Queen's Chambers have angled shafts, which may have been used as ventilation ducts, but are more likely to have been built for ceremonial purposes. They are oriented precisely toward Orion and the Pole Star, revealing the astronomical expertise of the builders. The original pyramid was covered by polished white limestone casing stones, which were loosened by earthquakes over the centuries and taken away as building materials in Cairo.

Location Giza, Egypt

Style Egyptian stepped pyramid

Purpose Burial chamber and spiritual center

Materials Limestone and granite, finished with polished white limestone and a granite capstone.

Area Originally 755.8 sq ft (230.4 sq m); now 745 sq ft (227 sq m)

Angle of incline 51 degrees

Cost to build About 1600 talents

Weight About 6 million tons (5,443108 tonnes)

Number of visitors per year ‼ = up to 1 million	Number of years to build Ţ = 1 year	Height of the structure
👣👣👣 3 million visitors	20 years	450 ft (137.2m)

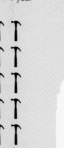

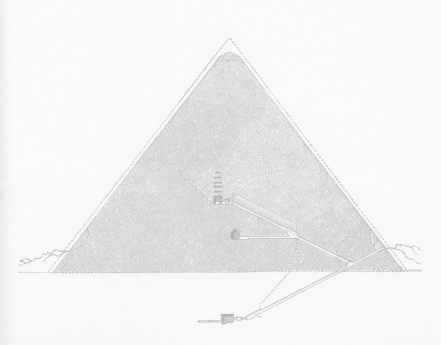

This cross-section of the Great Pyramid shows the ascending passage inside, which leads to the King's and Queen's Chambers. This is the only known ascending system to have a Grand Gallery. The descending passage leads to subterranean chambers.

Pyramids of Giza The Model

Origami Architect María Victoria Garrido Bianchini

Difficulty Level Easy

This card really captures the spirit of these gargantuan monuments to the ancient pharaohs and queens they entombed. Even using thin material like paper, you can still appreciate the immense weight of the actual pyramids' stone slabs, just imagine holding tons instead of ounces! (*See template on page 73.*)

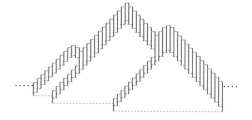

1 With the printed side of the template facing you, gently push back the valley folds at the base of the pyramids. Don't work the length of the fold lines; do just enough to lightly form the fold.

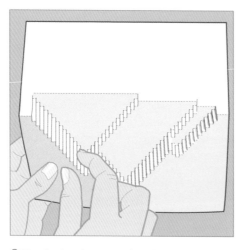

2 Turn the template around, and push back the valley folds on the steps of the three pyramids. You will notice that the mountain folds naturally follow.

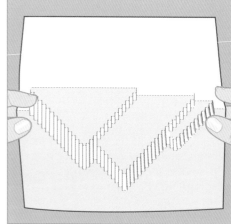

3 Holding the template with both hands, with the thumbs and index fingers above and the rest of your fingers below the paper, gently fold the gutter line up a little, but not completely.

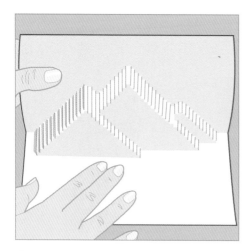

4 Turn the template over so that you are now looking at the unprinted side of the paper. Holding the template with one hand on the base of the pyramids, use your other hand to push from the back of the card toward you.

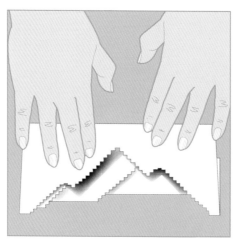

5 Turn the template over once again, so that you are now looking at the printed side. Use both hands to slowly close the card along its center, ensuring that all the folds are correctly positioned. Press down firmly on a flat surface, then open up to display your model.

London Eye **The Model**

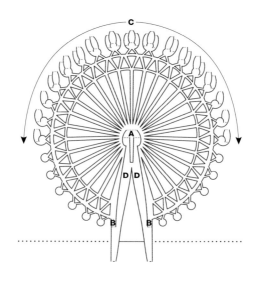

Origami Architect Ingrid Siliakus

Difficulty Level Easy

This project is largely about the cutting rather than the folding. If you want to practice your cutting skills, then this is the project for you. There are lots of small areas and rounded shapes to cut out. In contrast, there are not many folding lines. Once you've cut the card, you're almost there. (*See template on page 75.*)

1 Looking at the unprinted side of the template, with one hand on the front and one on the back, push the gutter fold down while simultaneously pushing the wheel forward. Do this for the gutter fold on the left and right sides. Stop when the gutter fold is at an angle of about 45 degrees.

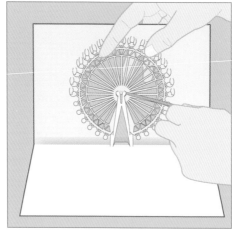

2 Insert a bamboo skewer behind the mountain folds in **Region A**, and use it to pull them to the front. It helps to hold the area above these folding lines with your other hand, close to the lines on which you are working. Keep this area steady while you pull **Region A** toward you.

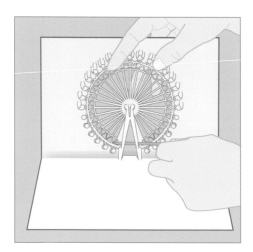

3 Use the skewer between the mountain fold and valley folds of **Region B**. Pull this area to the front, to bring the mountain folds into shape. Push the valley folds to the back, while simultaneously squeezing the folds between the finger and thumb of your hand on the back, one at a time.

4 Starting at the top, put the bamboo skewer behind each mountain fold in **Region C**, and pull them to the front and upward. Hold the upper part of the card steady with one hand. Repeat all previous steps until all folds are almost fully formed and the card can be put up at a 90-degree angle.

5 Use thumbs and index fingers on both sides of **Region D** and tilt it up, squeezing the mountain folds in **Region A** into shape. Keep one finger at the back of **Region A** while you bring it into shape. You will notice that the fold lines located in **Region B** can be brought into shape as well.

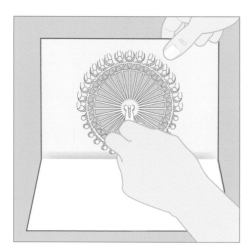

6 Hold the lower part of the wheel—first on one side then on the other—and tilt it up, so that the folds in **Region C** take shape. Keep repeating all steps, easing the folds further into shape, until the card can be closed entirely. Press down on the closed card, then open up to display your model.

London Eye Built *1998–1999* CE

Architects **David Marks and Julia Barfield of Marks Barfield Architects**

Location London, U.K.

Style Contemporary

Purpose Observation tower

Materials Steel, glass, and concrete

Cost to build £70 million

Weight 2,315 tons (2,100 tonnes)

Wheel circumference 1,392 ft (424m)

Capsules 32

Passengers 800 total; 25 per capsule

The London Eye, or Millennium Wheel, opened to the public on March 1, 2000 as an observation wheel and tourist attraction on the south bank of the Thames River, between London's Westminster Bridge and Hungerford Bridge. It was erected next to the site of the 1951 Festival of Britain and it gives visitors a bird's-eye view of the city. At 443 feet (135m), it is the tallest Ferris wheel in Europe—although no longer the tallest in the world, that being the 541-foot (165-m) Singapore Flyer, which opened in 2008—and the busiest ticketed tourist attraction in Britain.

The London Eye looks like a vast bicycle wheel in motion, complete with rim and spokes. Suspended from the outside of the main rim are 32 oval capsules—representing London's 32 boroughs—which passengers step into as the wheel moves slowly around. The wheel makes two rotations an hour thanks to hydraulic drive wheels.

Assembly of the wheel itself began on pontoons in the Thames in 1999. The pieces were then lifted into position by a crane at the rate of two degrees an hour. The entire Eye weighs 1,700 tons (1,542 tonnes) but it would be much heavier without using steel cables as its spokes, including 16 rim rotation cables and 64 spoke cables. The hub is made from eight sections of a hollow rolled steel tube, again keeping the structure lighter than it would have been if it were constructed with solid pieces.

The main support is a steel A-frame, which sits behind the wheel and on one side. It allows the operators (originally British Airways) to claim that the London Eye is the "world's tallest cantilevered observation wheel." On the other side, the A-frame receives support from six backstay cables, which hold the wheel more firmly in position. The cables are linked to a series of concrete piles, buried 108 feet (33m) underground for additional support.

Number of visitors per year
!! = up to 1 million

Number of years to build
T = 1 year

Height of the structure

1 year

442.9 ft (135m)

30.8 million visitors

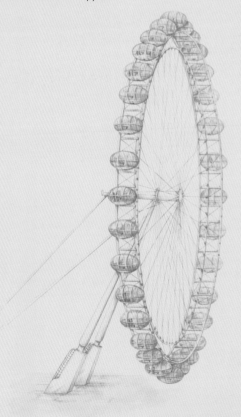

A graphic representation of the Eye. Each of the 32 egg-shaped capsules can accommodate up to 25 passengers and they travel at a sedate speed of 0.6 miles (0.9km) per hour.

Chichén Itzá Built *approx. 800–1200* CE

Architects **Unknown**

Chichén Itzá is a Maya site in the Yucatán, Mexico, and was an important and powerful Mesoamerican city between 800 and 1200 CE. Its ruins include temples, palaces, ball courts, and other buildings, which encompass various styles from that period but are predominantly Maya-Toltec (approx. 950–1200). The whole site is dominated by the Temple of Kukulkán (El Castillo), a pyramid with steps up to the summit, which is dedicated to one of the favorite gods of the Toltec, known as Quetzalcoatl (the plumed serpent).

The complex includes a smaller pyramid (known as the Temple of the Warriors), the Plaza of a Thousand Columns, an old market place, and a rounded Caracol (Snail) observatory. The observatory features a spiral stone staircase with openings oriented to the vernal equinox. Other buildings include the governmental palace Las Monjas ("Nunnery"), the Red House, the House of the Deer, the Ossuary, and the Sacred Cenote. Chichén Itzá was abandoned around 1400 CE—though nobody knows why—and the center of Mayan civilization shifted to Mayapán.

The Temple of Kukulkán is a vast, stepped pyramid with stairways on all four sides up to a temple. At mid-afternoon during the spring and fall equinoxes, it casts a large shadow shaped like a plumed serpent. Serpent carvings predominate in an edifice of corbelled vaulting and large rooms.

The Great Ball Court is one of the most impressive aspects of the whole site, and the most extraordinary of all the Mesoamerican ball courts. Its high walls slant at the foot to keep the ball in play, and the circular goals high in the walls on both the long sides are carved with serpents.

Location Southern Campeche, Yucatán, Mexico

Style Classic Maya, Maya-Toltec

Purpose Maya city

Materials Stone

Area 6 sq miles (15.5 sq km)

Decoration Frescoes and sculptures

Number of visitors per year
👣 = up to 1 million

👣👣👣
more than 1 million visitors

Number of years to build
🕐 = up to 20 years

Height of the structure

400 years

75 ft (22.8m)

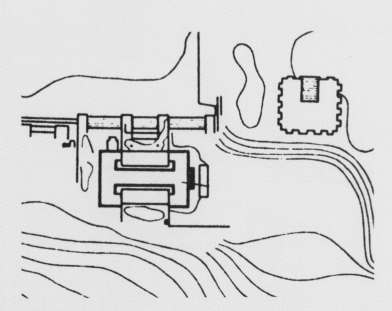

An aerial view of the Great Ball Court at Chichén Itzá, a large masonry structure with long, narrow alleys. At 202 yards (185m) long and 71 yards (65m) wide, it is larger than a modern American football field and the largest known Mesoamerican ball court in existence.

Chichén Itzá The Model

 Origami Architect María Victoria Garrido Bianchini

 Difficulty Level Easy

This South American pyramid was designed vertically in relation to the central gutter. The folding process in this model has to be progressive. This means that you will not fold any line to the end. Just keep folding them a little, go to a different line, then come back to the previous one, working on all the lines of the model almost at the same time. (*See template on page 77.*)

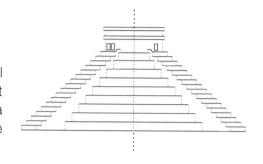

1 Holding the template so that you are looking at the printed side, push back the valley folds on the thinner steps.

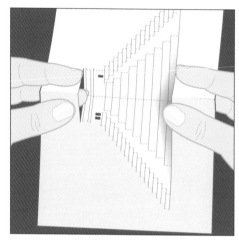

2 Fold down the gutter line just enough to mark the fold. At the same time, fold the valley lines at the top of the pyramid. Next, work on the second flight of thinner steps by pushing back the valley lines as in step 1.

3 Turn the template over so that you are looking at the unprinted side. Holding it in one hand, use your other hand to push the inner wall of the smaller stairs out, as if trying to join your hands together. Rotate the template and work on the other flight of smaller stairs.

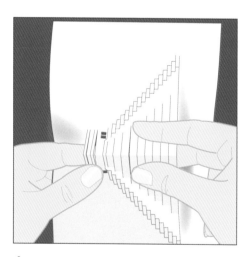

4 Push the mountain fold in the center of the pyramid toward you, just enough to form the fold.

5 Turn the template over once again, so that you are looking at the printed side. Push back the valley folds on the larger flights of steps at either side of the pyramid. At the same time, fold the mountain lines in the center of the pyramid.

6 Now use both hands to slowly close the card along the center, ensuring that all folds are correct. Once you are sure of this, place the closed card on a flat surface and press down firmly. Open up to display your model.

Seagram Building The Model

 Origami Architect María Victoria Garrido Bianchini

★ **Difficulty Level** Easy

This origami version of Mies van der Rohe's elegant skyscraper is highly effective. It even follows the principles of his famous design philosophy: "less is more" and "structure is spiritual." The hallmarks of his building style are extreme clarity and simplicity, and these are reflected here. If you are not yet confident at cutting small areas, you can leave the windows or paint them gray. (*See template on page 79.*)

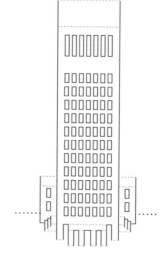

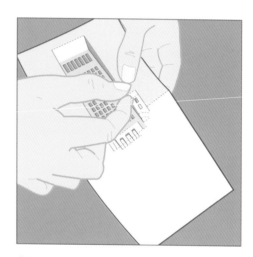

1 With the printed side of the template facing up, push back the valley fold at the base of the building—just enough to mark the fold. Do the same with the steps, being particularly careful because this area of the model is delicate.

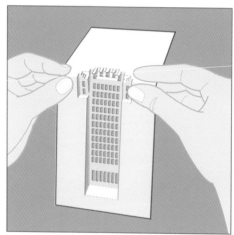

2 Holding the template with both hands, with the thumbs and index fingers above and the rest of your fingers below the paper, fold the gutter line upward slightly. Also fold the valley lines on the roofs of the small buildings at either side of the central tower.

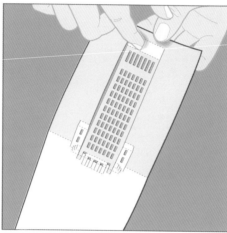

3 Turn the template 180 degrees, and push back the valley folds on the roof of the tower.

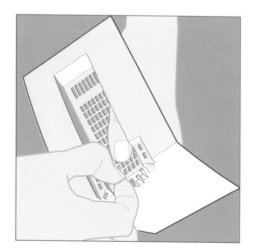

4 Holding the template with one hand at the base of the tower, fold back the valley lines on the roof above the columns at the foot of the tower. The mountain lines will fold automatically.

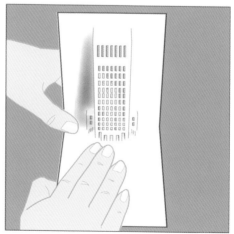

5 Turn the template over so that you are looking at the unprinted side. With one hand holding the base of the tower, use your other hand to push from the back of the card toward you. Be very careful when doing this to the columns on the front door.

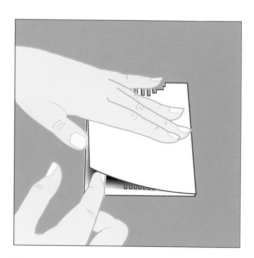

6 Slowly close the card along the center, ensuring that all folds are correctly positioned. Once you are sure of this, place the closed card on a flat surface, and press down firmly. Open up to display your model.

Seagram Building Built *1954–1958 CE*

Architect **Ludwig Mies van Der Rohe**

Associate architects **Kahn & Jacobs, Philip Johnson**

 Location New York City, U.S.A.

 Style Modernist, International

 Purpose Office building

 Materials Steel, glass, bronze, travertine, and marble

 Area 11,985 sq ft (1,118 sq m)

Decoration Bronze mullions and spandrels

 Cost to build $36 million

When Canadian distiller Joseph E. Seagram's & Sons required a new headquarters building in New York City in 1954, it commissioned the pioneering German-American modernist Ludwig Mies van der Rohe (1886–1969). His Seagram Building on Park Avenue eventually cost $36 million (equivalent to about $280 billion today) and was the most expensive skyscraper that had ever been built. The 515-foot (157-m) tower has thirty-eight stories in a rectangular steel-framed building, standing on granite pillars. Out front is a plaza that is graced with a number of trees, two pools, and a low boundary wall made of marble. The building itself is geometrically simple; it has become one of the most important Modernist buildings ever built and an icon of the International style (the expansion of iconic unornamented buildings using the ideas of the Modern Movement). Philip Johnson (1906–2005), a colleague of Mies's, collaborated with him on the interior—notably the Four Seasons restaurant, the world-famous Manhattan dining destination located in the building.

Although it has little ornamentation, the building is striking due to the alternating bands of bronze plating and bronze-tinted glass that cover the exterior. New York building codes required structural steel to be covered with fireproof material, usually concrete, but Mies wanted the steel structure to be visible. His creative solution was to use bronze-colored beams. The beams emphasize the building's height and appear to be structural, even though their purpose is purely decorative.

The window blinds are another unusual feature of the building. Mies did not want the windows to look irregular when the blinds were all drawn by different inhabitants at different heights; this would go against the clean, Modernist aesthetic of the rest of the building. To resolve this problem, he installed special blinds that have only three positions: open, half-open, and closed. These clean horizontal lines add to the organization of the building's façade when it is viewed from outside because the windows themselves go from floor to ceiling, covering entire walls.

Number of office workers
⁝⁝ = up to 1 million

⁝⁝ 5,000 office workers

Number of years to build
T = 1 year

T T
T T
4 years

Height of the structure

515 ft (157 m)

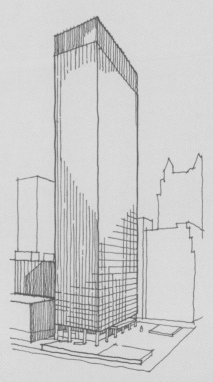

The Seagram Building was the first building constructed with floor-to-ceiling windows. It comprises a tall, rectilinear structure of 38 stories with a four-story extension at the rear.

Eiffel Tower Built *1887–1889* CE

Architect **Stephen Sauvestre**

Engineers **Emile Nouguier, Maurice Koechlin**

Contractor **Gustave Eiffel & Cie**

The Eiffel Tower stands on the left bank of the Seine River in Paris, flanking the Champ de Mars. It was conceived as the entrance arch for the Exposition Universelle (World Fair) of 1889 and built to mark the centenary of the French Revolution. The architect and bridge engineer Gustave Eiffel (1832–1923) secured a twenty-year permit for the structure to remain standing, despite the protests against his use of exposed wrought-iron. Yet the building overcame the opposition, partly because of its symbolic status and partly because of its unexpected function: It could be used to transmit radio and television broadcasts. This was utilized in 1909 and 1957 respectively.

Construction began on July 1, 1887, when 18,038 iron pieces, calculated to a thousandth of an inch, were assembled into larger elements of 13–16 feet (4–5m) and secured together by millions of rivets. Thanks to the use of wooden scaffolding and steam cranes, construction was complete in just twenty-one months. It was the world's tallest tower and remained so until New York's Chrysler Building was completed in 1931.

The Eiffel Tower's basic structure combines a Roman triumphal arch and, because the tower soars to a point, what amounts to a Gothic spire. Four curved, tapering lattice-girder piers, aligned to the points of the compass, rise from the reinforced-concrete square base. The piers form arches under the first of four platforms. Stairs provide access to the first two platforms, but the upper platforms can be reached only by elevator.

Planning the structure required a small revolution in engineering. Eiffel used precise mathematical calculations to plan for the weight that the iron trusses and arches needed to support. To complicate matters, the tower had to be able to sway gently at its summit. He was able to achieve the mobility—and the building's unprecedented height—by using wrought-iron open latticework supported by girders. The glass-cased elevators, hauled by water-powered pistons, had to be designed to travel along the curve of the tower's legs.

Location Paris, France

Style Expressionist, Modernist

Purpose World's Fair entrance arch and observation tower

Materials Puddled wrought-iron, glass, and concrete

Area 412 sq ft (38 sq m)

Features 4 platforms, 3 elevators, and 1,652 steps

Decoration Exposed wrought-iron latticework

Cost to build 7.8 million francs

Weight 10,000 tons (9,072 tonnes)

Number of visitors per year
!! = up to 1 million

Number of years to build
T = 1 year

Height of the structure

2 years

7 million visitors

1,063 ft (325m)

The Eiffel Tower was a great feat of engineering built for the 1889 International Exhibition. It was assembled over two years, one section at a time, by over 300 steel workers.

Eiffel Tower The Model

Origami Architect María Victoria Garrido Bianchini

Difficulty Level Easy

This 1,000-foot (300-m) high maiden of iron, calculated to dominate the city's skyline, has now become an iconic edifice. Its singular lines are unmistakable in the model. The origami design of this nineteenth-century symbol of innovative technical engineering boasts the beauty of the tower's latticework structure. (*See template on page 79.*)

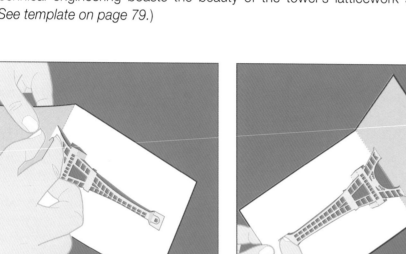

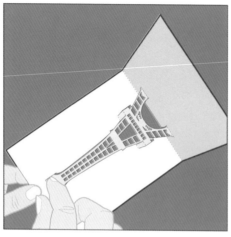

1 Looking at the printed side of the template, gently push the valley folds at the base of the tower legs toward you, so that you begin to mark the folds. Do not complete the folds at this stage.

2 Rotate the template, and continue in the same way with the valley folds at the top of the tower and in the middle of the structure. Continue turning the template and working on the valley folds.

3 Holding the template with both hands, with the thumbs and index fingers on top and the rest of your fingers below the paper, fold the gutter line upward a little, but again do not complete the fold at this stage.

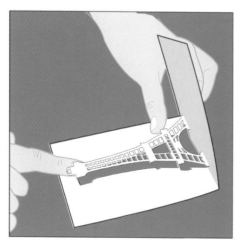

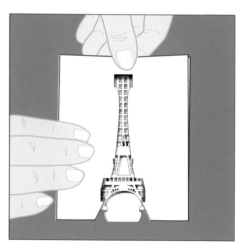

4 Turn the template over so that you are looking at the unprinted side. With one hand at the base of the tower area, use your other hand to gently push from the back toward you.

5 Position the card as shown, and gently press the valley folds on the back. Be especially careful when working the base of the legs, as this area is delicate.

6 Turn the card over again, then slowly close it along the center, ensuring that all the folds are correct. Place the card on a flat surface and press down firmly, then open up to display your model.

Parthenon The Model

 Origami Architect María Victoria Garrido Bianchini

★ **Difficulty Level** Easy

The temple of Athena Parthenos on the Acropolis in Athens was built 2,400 years ago. Most origami architects have chosen to replicate its original form, but here the design replicates the building as it is today. Despite the model reflecting the building's half-destroyed state, the dignity of what is reputedly the most perfect Doric temple ever constructed can still be clearly seen. (*See template on page 81.*)

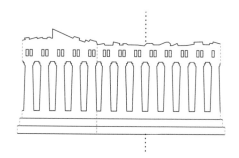

1 Looking at the printed side of the template, push back the valley folds on the steps and at the top of the building (the frieze).

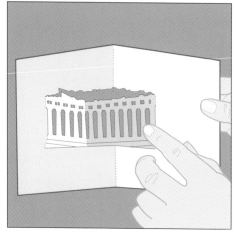

2 Do the same on the other side. Pay special attention to the thin steps at the base of the building as they are particularly delicate.

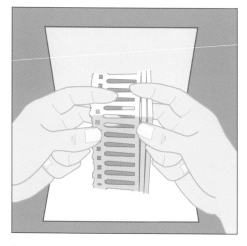

3 Turn the template over so that you are looking at the unprinted side. Holding the template with both hands, with the thumbs and index fingers above and the rest of your fingers below the paper, work on the mountain folds in the middle of the building, folding the lines upward.

4 Turn the template over again. Hold the template with both hands, with the thumbs and index fingers above and the rest of your fingers below the paper, and fold the central gutter line upward a little more.

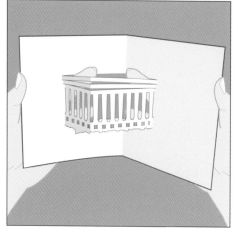

5 Turn the template over once more, and, with both hands, slowly close the card along the central gutter line, ensuring that all the folds are correct.

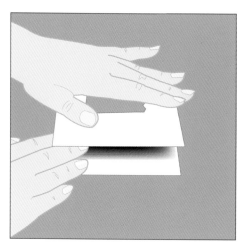

6 Place the closed card on a flat surface and press down firmly. Open up to display your model.

Parthenon Built *447–432* BCE
Architects **Iktinos and Kallikrates**

 Location Athens, Greece

 Style Exterior: Ancient Greek, Doric

 Purpose Temple

 Materials Marble, masonry, stone, gold, bronze, ivory, glass, ebony, and cypress

 Area 23,028 sq ft (2,148 sq m)

 Decoration Gold, ivory, friezes, and sculptures

 Cost to build 469 silver talents

The Parthenon is part of the Acropolis complex in Athens, originally built as a temple to the goddess Athena. It is the most important surviving building of ancient Greece and a symbol of Athenian democracy. The marble temple was commissioned at the height of Athens' importance as a cultural center (around 447 BCE) by the Athenian statesman Pericles. The task of his architects, Iktinos and Kallikrates, was to extend an earlier temple burned by the Persians. By 432 BCE, the building had been completed.

The Parthenon was unusual: It was a Doric temple with some Ionic interior features, including slender columns and Ionic orders in the opisthodomos (back room). It has also had a checkered history. This masterpiece of classical architecture has been a Christian church, a mosque, and a Turkish munitions store.

The static design is made to seem more alive by a series of gentle curves. Although the columns lean slightly inward, they look as if they are leaning slightly outward because of their strange, cigarlike shape. The west front was also built slightly higher than the east, and the end columns are larger and closer together. Similar curves are found in the platform on which the columns stand (the stylobate), the posts on either side of the doorway (the antae), and on the moldings above the columns (the entablature), all of which gives a sense of organic movement.

There are six Doric columns supporting the front and back porches and twenty-three smaller Doric columns surrounding Athena's statue in the inner chamber (the cella). Scholars disagree whether the cella was fully roofed or not, but most concur that the decorations, carvings, and friezes around the walls and in the cella were originally brightly colored. The colors suggest that despite its religious origins the Parthenon may also have been used as a treasury.

Number of visitors per year
‼ = up to 1 million

Number of years to build
Ʇ = 1 year

Height of the structure

3 million visitors

15 years

64 ft (19.5m)

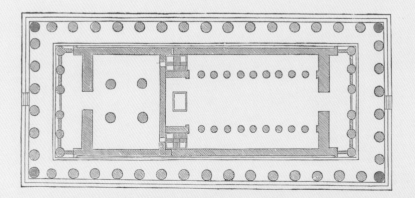

This floor plan shows the Parthenon's rectangular shape. It is surrounded by a colonnade of Doric columns, with an extra six columns in front of each entrance. Each side has a series of low steps.

Colosseum *Built approx. 70–80 CE*

Architect **Unknown**

The vast, elliptical Colosseum, used for five centuries as the heart of Roman entertainment, is now a partial ruin in the center of Rome. It began life as the Flavian Amphitheater, started by the Emperor Vespasian (9–79 CE), and it was finished by his son Titus in 80 CE. Based on the amphitheaters of ancient Greece, it was used for gladiatorial contests, fights between men and animals, mock battles, and classical dramas until the sixth century. Later it was used for housing, religious rituals, and as a fortress. The Colosseum is shaped as an ellipse, 615 feet (189m) long, with an oval arena in the center surrounded by tiers of seating for up to 50,000 people. The seating has long since disappeared, but the basic shape remains and the corridors and spaces below the arena are now open to the air. The original interior also featured corridors, stairways, ramps, and gates through which spectators went to their seats. Subterranean tunnels contained machinery and sets, cages for gladiators and animals, and eighty vertical shafts to transport items to the surface.

The Colosseum arena was originally surrounded by a wall, above which rose tiered seating in stone and marble. The first tier was set aside for senators and the most important members of Roman society, with a special box in prime position for the emperor and reserved seating for the vestal virgins. What remains of the outer wall's façade includes three layers of round-arched arcades framed by engaged half-columns: Doric-Tuscan, then Ionic, and Corinthian. Natural light floods through the arches, giving the impression of both lightness and strength. The fourth story—above the main seating—had Corinthian pilasters, small windows, and galleries with simple wooden benches, designed to contain the less-favored spectators, among them women, the common poor, and slaves.

The original structure included a series of stone ledges on the top of the walls, which supported beams and held a series of awnings (velariums) to afford the crowd protection from the sun. The awnings covered about two-thirds of the stadium with the help of large canvas coverings, which were so unwieldy that they needed to be hauled into place by up to a hundred Romans.

Location Rome, Italy

Style Doric, Ionic, and Corinthian

Purpose Public arena

Materials Concrete, brick, marble, travertine, tufa, and wood

Area 313,650 sq ft (29,371 sq m)

Features 240 round arches; 480 Doric-Tuscan, Ionic, and Corinthian half-columns; and 80 entrances

Number of visitors per year
👣 = up to 1 million

4 million visitors

Number of years to build
T = 1 year

10 years

Height of the structure

159 ft (48.5m)

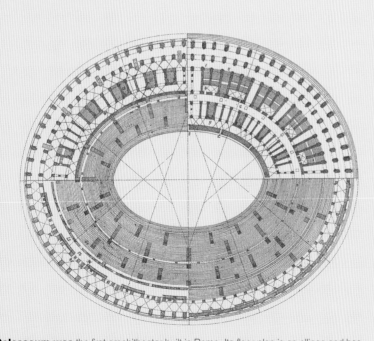

The Colosseum was the first amphitheater built in Rome. Its floor plan is an ellipse and has 80 supporting walls radiating outward. The whole structure covers approximately 6 acres (2.4 ha).

Colosseum The Model

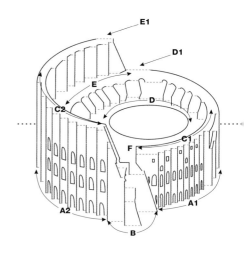

Origami Architect Ingrid Siliakus

Difficulty Level Easy

The folding stage of this project is fairly simple; however, the initial cutting is more challenging. The many rounded windows and doors at the front of the template, which are all very close to the straight cutting lines, are quite difficult. Remember, it is best to start with the interior cutting lines, before moving on to the exterior lines. (*See template on page 83.*)

1 Holding the template with the unprinted side facing you, use one hand to fold the gutter line on the right. With the other, push behind **Region A1**, and press the gutter line in. Avoid **Region F** giving a false crease. Rotate the card 180 degrees and repeat for **A2**. Rotate the card back.

2 Press your thumb from the back of the card through the center hole. With your other hand, hold the empty area under **Region B**. Push carefully toward the thumb in the hole, and use that thumb to push the middle part down a little to shape the mountain folds of **Region B**.

3 Hold **Region C1** and fold it down, to shape the mountain fold lines, at the same time pushing this entire area toward your thumb on the front of the card. With the thumb and index finger of your other hand, working from the front, take hold of **Region C2** and push it down to shape the mountain folds.

4 Run your nails in to the valley folds of **Region D**. Press them inward, squeezing your fingers on the back of the card directly above and below. Repeat for **D1**. Repeat for **E** and the valley fold marked **E1**. Repeat steps 1–4, folding everything a little further inward or outward.

5 Repeat steps 1–4, pressing your nails into the mountain folds of **D** and **E**, while pushing your fingers directly above and below from the other side of the card. Repeat steps 1–4 on all valley and mountain folds on both sides, until this section (**D** and **E**) of the card is shaped.

6 Look for areas that are too rigid for the card to close. Pinch mountain fold lines together while pushing against the upper part of the card. For areas **D** and **E**, put a finger through the center hole and push up and back. For areas **A** and **B**, press against the valley fold lines from the back.

Golden Pavilion The Model

 Origami Architect Ingrid Siliakus

 Difficulty Level Easy

A bamboo skewer is recommended for this project; it will really help you get the beautiful curved roofs into shape. Insert the skewer behind the middle mountain fold lines of the roofs. When you tilt them toward you, the other curved lines of the roof should form, too. Keep in mind that the central mountain folds between the two vertical gutter lines are the key to success. (*See template on page 85.*)

1 Looking at the unprinted side of the template, hold it with one hand on the back and one on the front. Press the gutter fold into shape a little, while pushing the model forward slightly using the hand on the back.

2 Next, concentrate on the outer valley folds on the left and right sides of the model, pushing them backward into shape.

3 As you work on folding these first lines, other areas of the model also tend to get into shape. Turn your attention to those areas, and encourage the valley/mountain folds into shape by working them with one hand on the back of the template and one on the front.

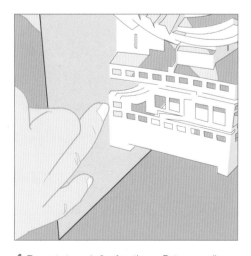

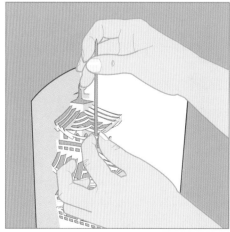

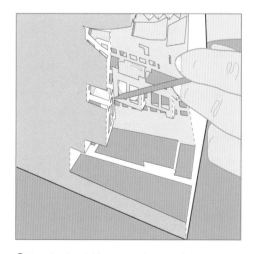

4 Repeat steps 1–3 a few times. Put your nails into the valley folds located at the outer left and right sides of the model, to maneuver these lines further into shape. At the same time, squeeze these fold lines using the thumb and index finger of your hand on the back of the card.

5 Place a skewer behind each center mountain fold. As you tilt the mountain folds toward you, squeeze into shape with the thumb and index finger of your free hand. Start from the bottom and work your way up. Repeat this step a few times, then do the same for all the other mountain folds.

6 For all valley folds except those at the outer left and right, put a nail into the line on the front and pinch either side from the back. Or, you can turn the card to the back and use a skewer as you did in step 5. Repeat all steps until the card can be folded closed. Open up to display your model.

Golden Pavilion Built *1397 CE, reconstructed 1955*
Architect **Ashikaga Yoshimitsu**

Location Kyoto, Japan

Style Exterior: Shinden-zukuri (Heian period)

Purpose Zen temple

Materials Wood and lacquer

Area 1,320 sq ft (152 sq m)

Decoration Gold leaf, Japanese lacquer

The Temple of the Golden Pavilion (Kinkaku-ji)—also known as the Deer Park Temple (Rokuon-ji)—is one of the most revered medieval buildings in Japan. It owes its existence to the shogun Ashikaga Yoshimitsu (1358–1408), who started the building in 1397 as part of his retirement estate. After his death, the villa and its surrounding gardens were converted into a Zen Buddhist temple complex, which serves as the last resting place of a number of sacred relics of the Buddha. Throughout its history the temple has been burned down a number of times, most recently in 1950, which explains why the present structure dates from 1955.

The temple itself has three floors, each one designed in a different style. The first floor, known as the Hosui-in (Chamber of Dharma Waters), is in the shinden-zukuri style. The style's combination of aristocratic palace, courtyard, and pond, flourished in tenth-century Japan. This floor also includes a large room for greeting guests and a veranda.

The second floor contains Cho-on-do (Hall of Roaring Waves), in the buke-zukuri style of samurai houses. Buke-zukuri is known for compactness and a mixture of asymmetrical styles. The compact rooms on this floor were an ideal place for Yoshimitsu to spend time with his most honored guests.

The top floor, which is covered in gold leaf, is known as Kukkyo-cho (Firmament Top). It is built in karayo style (Zen temple style), which is based on extreme simplicity and is deliberately designed to encourage calmness. It has a floor space of only 23 square feet (7sq m) and is used for tea ceremonies and intimate meetings with friends. The windows are bell-shaped, set just below a small roof made from thin boards of Japanese cypress. The roof has a distinctively Japanese form and is crowned with a gilded phoenix.

Number of visitors per year
!! = up to 1 million

Number of years to build
T = 1 year

Height of the structure

1 year

25 million visitors

42 ft (12.8m)

Illustration showing the top floor of the Golden Pavilion, which has a pyramidlike structure. The top two floors are covered with gold leaf that gleams in the evening sun.

Sydney Opera House Built *1957–1973* CE

Architect **Jørn Utzon**

Engineers **Ove Arup & Partners**

Sydney Opera House is built on Bennelong Point in Sydney Harbour, Australia. It is an internationally recognizable example of Expressionist architecture—the movement known for buildings with distorted, fragmented, or romantic shapes—and is included on UNESCO's World Heritage List. The opera house was designed in 1957 by the Danish architect Jørn Utzon (1918–) and incorporates a series of roofs in groups of interlocking shells, all of which rest on a huge platform surrounded by terraces.

Before construction of the building could begin, concrete piers needed to be sunk below sea level to support the building's weight. The upper podium was built between 1959 and 1963, followed by the outer shells from 1963 to 1967. By 1966, the venture had vastly exceeded its budget and Utzon resigned after disagreements with presiding politicians.

The ballooning cost was partly due to a number of engineering challenges owing to the exposed site; Utzon needed to constantly rework his original design with Danish engineer Ove Arup. For example, it was not until 1961 that he solved the problem of how to avoid building each part of the shell roofs separately. One of the first exercises in computerized architecture provided the solution: Each roof section could be cast off-site as a section of a sphere. Each shell section was then held together by a precast concrete rib. Roof sections were joined together by tensioned steel cables, with a million glossy white and matte cream tiles covering the roof.

The interior—which contains two main halls, five theaters, five rehearsal studios, four restaurants, and six bars and stores—was constructed from 1967 to 1973. It is now home to Opera Australia, The Australian Ballet, Sydney Theatre Company, the Sydney Symphony, the Australian Chamber Orchestra, and various touring companies. The high cost of Utzon's interior plan was among the issues that led to his departure, and the decoration for the nearly 1,000 rooms changed to include mainly pink granite, wood, and brush box plywood. The vast amount of glass in the final building was also not part of Utzon's original building plans. However, in 2004 an interior space called the Utzon Room was rebuilt to match his original design and, in 2007, Utzon himself proposed a reconstruction of the Opera Theatre, which is still under discussion.

Location Sydney, Australia

Style Expressionist

Purpose Performance space

Materials Tile-clad and precast concrete, granite, steel, glass, and wood

Area 238,551 ft (22,200 sq m)

Cost to build AUS$102 million

Roof tiles More than 1 million

Glass 67,005 sq ft (6,225 sq m)

Features 1,000 rooms and 5,486 seats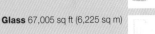

Number of visitors per year
!! = up to 1 million

Number of years to build
T =1 year

Height of the structure

4.5 million visitors

15 years

220 ft (67m)

Utzon's groundbreaking design for the Sydney Opera House utilizes a series of ribbed shells and spherical, freestanding roofs, reflecting his wish to create a "living sculpture."

Sydney Opera House The Model

 Origami Architect María Victoria Garrido Bianchini

★★ **Difficulty Level** Intermediate

Designed by the Danish architect Jørn Utzon, the Sydney Opera House constitutes a masterpiece of twentieth-century architecture. For this origamic version, the half-cutting has to be precise; therefore, it is imperative you use a metal ruler to guide you, especially to half-cut the steps close to the water. (*See template on page 87.*)

1 Looking at the printed side of the card, push back the valley folds at the base of the building. Do not push along the complete length of the lines; do just enough to mark the folds.

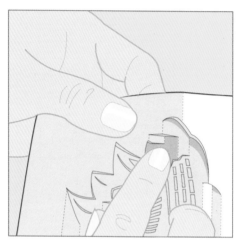

2 Turn the card around. Push back the valley folds at the top of the building and between the roofs. Also fold the valley lines on the two extremes of the building.

3 Holding the template with both hands, with the thumbs and index fingers above and the rest of your fingers below the paper, fold the central gutter line upward a little, but not to the end.

4 Make the mountain folds at the base of the building first, then work on the mountain folds on the roofs.

5 Turn the template over so that you are looking at the unprinted side of the paper. With one hand holding the base of the building, use your other hand to push from the back of the card toward you. Be very careful when folding the base of the building.

6 Now, with both hands, slowly close the card along the center, ensuring that all folds are correct. Once you are sure, place the card on a flat surface and press down firmly. Open up to display your model.

White House The Model

Origami Architect María Victoria Garrido Bianchini

Difficulty Level Intermediate

The White House model uses the 180-degree technique, combining two templates to form the finished building. When the card is opened to 180 degrees, the building pops up; whereas all the other models in this book are designed to be opened at 90 degrees. Make sure you only use the slightest amount of glue, otherwise the model will not fold properly. (*See templates on pages 89 and 91.*)

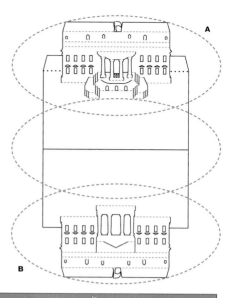

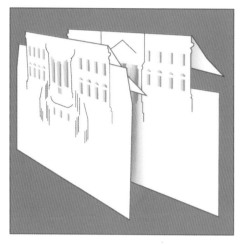

1 Hold template **A** so that you are looking at the unprinted side. With one hand on the balcony, bend the reverse side of it backward. Press firmly along the score lines and crease. Follow the same procedure with template **B**.

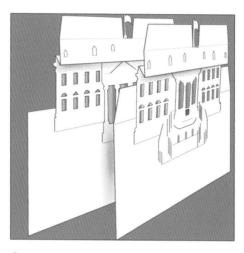

2 Turn template **A** over to the printed side and bend the half-roof toward you. Do the same with template **B**.

3 Apply a small amount of glue to the area between the two folds you have just made. Fold the roof on template **A** over the balcony and press together until the glue dries. Repeat with template **B**, but do not glue the area of the portico roof.

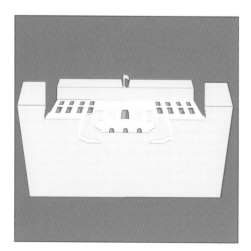

4 Still looking at the printed side of template **A**, gently push the valley folds backward so that you start to mark the folds. Be especially careful while folding the steps on template **A**. Follow the same procedure with template **B**.

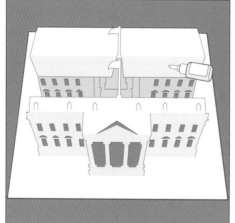

5 Align the back of template **A** with the back of template **B**. Apply glue to one of the roof tabs, and join both pieces. Apply glue to one of the flags and join both flags together. Turn both templates over, so that you are looking at the printed side, and push out all the chimneys.

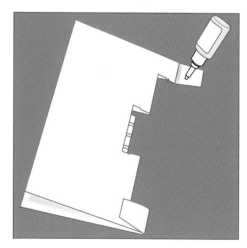

6 Fold the joined templates flat. Be sure to align the borders of both templates. Apply glue on the tabs as shown and fold over. Press firmly until the glue dries. Open up to display your model.

White House Built *1792–1800* CE

Architects **James Hoban** (1792), **Benjamin Latrobe** (1803), **McKim, Mead & White** (1901), **Nathan Wyeth** (1909)

 Location Washington DC, U.S.A.

 Style Exterior: Late Georgian, Palladian, Neoclassic

 Purpose President's mansion (originally called the President's Palace or Executive Mansion)

 Materials Sandstone, brick, plaster, marble, steel, wood, and glass

 Area 14,280 sq ft (1,331 sq m)

 Features 132 rooms, 35 bathrooms, 412 doors, 147 windows, 28 fireplaces, and 8 staircases

 Cost to build $232,400

As the first president of the United States, George Washington planned to use the building now known as the White House as a "President's Palace." Yet he never lived in it himself—partly because he was disappointed by the size of the winning design in his competition, drawn up by the Irish architect James Hoban (1758–1831)—and he ordered that the building be enlarged by a third. It has functioned as the presidential residence and staff offices since his successor, John Adams, moved there in 1800. The building occupies a focal point at the heart of the capital city that bears Washington's name. Nearly every president since Adams has altered the design, although the white color has remain unchanged. Notable additions include the West Wing (Theodore Roosevelt, 1902), which now houses the offices of the president and his staff, and the Oval Office (William Howard Taft, 1909), which is the most famous room in the West Wing.

Some of the biggest alterations were made when Thomas Jefferson moved into the White House in 1801, of which the East and West colonnades are now the most obvious. Designed originally in part to hide stables and outbuildings, they were constructed in 1803 as walkways lined by columns. While the East Colonnade was demolished in 1859, it was rebuilt in 1902 on the same foundations.

The distinctive north and south porticoes were constructed in the 1820s, replacing a series of wooden colonnades that had also been designed to hide the stables. Their white columns evoke Palladian mansions in Ireland or French chateaus, although both of these influences remain disputed because no evidence has been found that architect Benjamin Henry Latrobe had ever been to either country. Jefferson himself, however, had traveled there, and he is known to have influenced many aspects of the designs as they developed.

Number of visitors per year •• = up to 1 million
•••••• 2 million visitors

Number of years to build T = 1 year
8 years

Height of the structure
70 ft (21.3m)

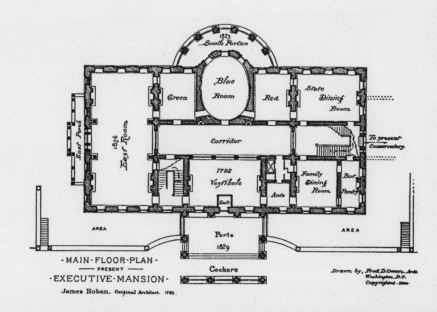

The original James Hoban design for a presidential palace. The design was subsequently enlarged by 30 percent, and a large reception hall—the East Room—was added.

Taj Mahal Built *1631–1653* CE

Architects **Ustad Ahmad Lahawri with Abd al-Karim Ma'Mur Khan, Makramat Khan, Ismail Afandi**

The Mogul emperor Shah Jahan built the marble Taj Mahal as a mausoleum beside the Yamuna River for his beloved wife, Mumtaz Mahal. It is the finest example of Mogal architecture, which combined Islamic, Persian, Indian, and Turkish styles. The mausoleum and its platform took twelve years to complete (1631–1643); workers had to haul the marble blocks up scaffolding before lifting them into place. The rest of the Taj complex—which included a gateway, gardens, a mosque, and a guesthouse—took ten additional years.

At the base of the mausoleum is a white-marble square platform with ridged corners, which is supported by red sandstone. Four minarets with cupolas rise from the corners of the platform, an example of the Islamic elements that make up Mogal architecture. Inside the mausoleum is an octagonal hall with four smaller halls attached. Shah Jahan and his wife lie in a plain crypt beneath the hall; her tomb located at the exact center of the building, under a spectacular marble dome. This dome is in the shape of an onion and is decorated with a lotus. It has four smaller domes around it, reflecting the same shape, and on the very top of the main dome is a bronze crescent moon motif pointing to heaven. This motif is an example of the extraordinary mixture of Hindu and Persian imagery that is found throughout the Taj Mahal.

On its exterior, the Taj Mahal has four façades, each one with an iwan (a vast vaulted space open on one side) framed by friezes of calligraphy. These Mogal decorations—mainly letter forms because Islamic rules forbid human figures—are etched in jasper and inlaid in marble panels. The designs on the higher panels are larger, so that they can be read even from far away.

Location Agra, India

Style Mogal, Islamic

Purpose Mausoleum

Materials White marble, red sandstone, tile, stucco, jade

Area 592 sq ft (55 sq m)

Features 5 domes and 4 minarets

Decoration Inlaid gemstones, abstract carvings, and bronze and gold finials

Cost to build 31 million rupees

Number of visitors per year
‼ = up to 1 million

Number of years to build
Ⱦ = 1 year

Height of the structure

2.4 million visitors

200 ft (61m)

22 years

The Taj Mahal consists of an integrated system of symmetrical structures, with a multi-chambered, cube-shaped base and chamfered edges.

Taj Mahal The Model

Origami Architect Joyce Aysta

★★ **Difficulty Level** Intermediate

The domes and cupolas of the Taj Mahal are a good exercise in cutting curves. Take your time. Cutting the eight little towers at the top of the building may prove difficult; you can leave them out if you wish. The curved line at the base of the dome can either be drawn on or cut out; this extra detail gives depth to the dome. (*See template on page 93.*)

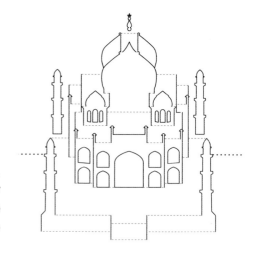

1 Holding the template at the bottom, looking at the unprinted side, gently push out the valley and mountain fold lines at the base of the model. Ease out the minarets on either side as you make the folds.

2 Next, start the gutter folds. As you make these, be sure that the minarets go through to the front of the card; they sometimes catch on the edges. Then turn your attention to the valley folds at the base of the buliding. This action will force the mountain folds at the top of the building.

3 Holding the card at the top, gently push out the valley folds at the top of the building and on the main dome.

4 Now work on the valley folds at the base of all three domes. This will force any remaining folds to form.

5 Slowly close the card completely, making sure that the small towers at the top corners and the large minarets in front don't catch on anything. Place the card on a flat surface and press down firmly. Open up to display your model.

Tower Bridge The Model

 Origami Architect María Victoria Garrido Bianchini

★★ **Difficulty Level** Intermediate

This bridge has many cut-outs. Make sure you use a metal ruler as a guide and start on the interior cuts, such as the windows and doors and the area at the top of the bridge, before moving on to the exterior cuts. If you are not yet confident cutting out very small pieces, you can leave the windows of the boat and keep it as a silhouette instead. *(See template on page 95.)*

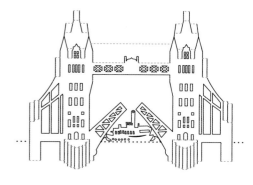

1 Looking at the printed side of the card, gently push the valley folds on the base of the towers backward, just enough to mark the folds.

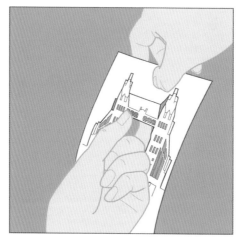

2 Turn the card around and continue in the same way with the valley folds at the top of the towers and the bridge. Continue turning the card as often as necessary and working gently on the valley folds.

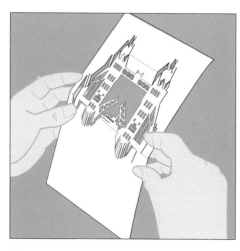

3 Now fold the central gutter line upward a little, using your thumbs and index fingers, with the rest of your fingers below the paper.

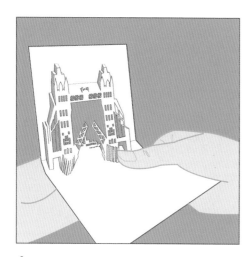

4 Turn the card over so that you are looking at the unprinted side. With one hand holding the base of the towers, use your other hand to push from the back of the card toward you. The mountain folds at the base will follow naturally.

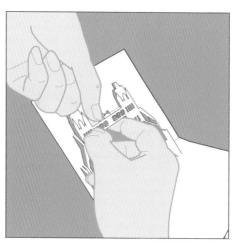

5 Now turn your attention to the mountain fold at the top of the bridge, pushing from the back of the card toward you.

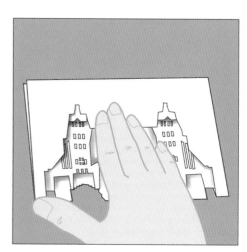

6 Turn the card over again and slowly close it along its center, gently completing the folds. Place the card on a flat surface and press down firmly. Next, fold the boat very carefully along the blue lines. Open up to display your model.

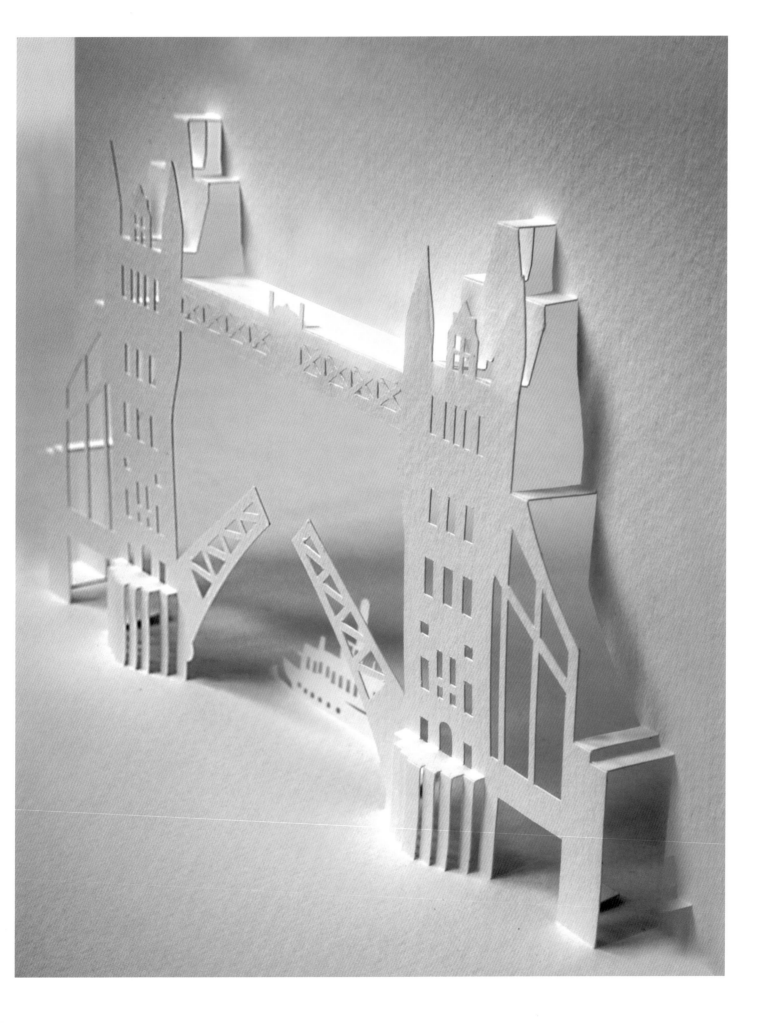

Tower Bridge Built *1886–1894* CE

Architects **Horace Jones and George D. Stevenson**
Engineer **John Wolfe Barry**

Location London, U.K.

Style Victorian Gothic

Purpose Road bridge and footbridge

Materials Cornish granite, Portland stone, cement, concrete, bricks, iron, steel, and glass

Area (main span) 38,000 sq ft (3,514 sq m)

Features 100 windows, 2 walkways, 2 piers, towers, 2 anchorages, and 2 bascules

Decoration Victorian Gothic-style brick facade

Cost to build £120,000

Tower Bridge lies east of the Tower of London on the Thames River and is the world's most famous example of a combined bascule (drawbridge) and suspension bridge. Its western neighbor, London Bridge, was once the city's only bridge over the Thames. While more bridges were built to the west as London expanded, a bridge to the east wasn't needed until London's East End began to develop in the late nineteenth century. The bridge was designed to ease traffic across the existing bridges, but it also needed to let shipping reach the docks at the Pool of London—between the Tower of London and London Bridge.

In 1884, City of London Architect Horace Jones (1819–1897) and the engineer John Wolfe Barry (1836–1918) designed the suspension bridge with two towers supported by massive concrete piers sunk into the river bed. When Jones died in 1897, engineer George D. Stevenson took over and changed the façade to a romantic Victorian version.

The central span of the bridge consists of two equal bascules (drawbridges with counterpoises) that are raised by hydraulic steam power to allow ships to pass below. The bascules have a two-lane roadway with a pedestrian walkway either side. The pinnacle-topped towers are made of steel, but are covered in Cornish granite and Portland stone to protect the steelwork and provide a romantic appearance that blends with the adjacent medieval Tower of London. Some critics have ridiculed the combination of Victorian engineering and medieval pastiche.

Between the towers and the river banks are suspension bridges that are anchored at the abutments and connected by rods into the upper walkways linking the two towers. These upper walkways, 143 feet (44m) above the high-tide level, were designed as a scenic route to be used when the bridge was open. They became a haunt for beggars and prostitutes, however, and the City of London authorities closed them in 1910. They were reopened in 1982 as an exhibition space and remain open to this day.

Number of vehicles per year
 = 5 million

Number of years to build
T = 1 year

Height of the structure

15 million vehicles

8 years

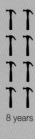

140 ft (42.7m) above water; 33 ft (11m) below water (high tide)

The innovative design of this bridge is based on two towers linked by a bridge beam, with a main suspension cable, suspending bars, and diagonal cable stays.

Taos Pueblo Built *1000–1450* CE

Architects **Unknown**

Taos Pueblo is the largest and most northern Native American settlement of its kind in New Mexico. Archaeologists date it somewhere between 1000 and 1450 CE, and it has been lived in—as far as we know—ever since then. That makes it the oldest continuously inhabited community in North America and the very earliest North American architecture still in existence.

Taos Pueblo is located a mile (0.6km) north of the modern city of Taos, on the Red Willow Creek, and at the heart of a reservation that is home to about 1,900 people; 150 people still live in the pueblo itself. A Roman Catholic chapel dedicated to St. Jerome, completed in 1850, is on the same site. It is the third church built on the reservation—the first was destroyed in 1680 and the second was a casualty of a siege by U.S. forces in 1847.

The main building of the pueblo, which is divided by the river, is a multilevel residential building constructed using adobe—a mixture of earth with straw and water—that is many feet thick in places. The five floors of dwellings are self-contained, built side by side in layers, with common walls but no connecting passageways. They typically consist of two rooms, one below for cooking, eating, and storage, and the other above for relaxing and sleeping.

The main purpose of the building's design was defensive, which is why the windows and the small low door openings in the lower floors were not built until around 1900. Until then, the main entrance to the homes was from above, with access to rooms on lower floors by ladder to the roof outside, then down an inside ladder. Large cedar logs support the roofs of each of the five floors and protrude through the walls.

Location Taos, New Mexico, U.S.A.

Style Southwest Vernacular

Purpose Multifamily dwelling

Materials Adobe brick (sun-dried mud, clay, straw, water), cedar, pine, and aspen

Area 15.6 sq miles (25.1 sq km)

Housing units 441

Population 150

Alterations Doors and windows added 1900

Number of inhabitants per year !! = up to 1 million — approx. 150 inhabitants

Number of years to build ① = up to 20 years — 450 years

Elevation of the village   Approx. 50 ft (15m)

The architectural style of Taos Pueblo is distinctive, with its multitude of stories built from reddish-brown adobe topped by flat roofs—the adobe walls can be several feet thick.

Taos Pueblo The Model

 Origami Architect María Victoria Garrido Bianchini

 Difficulty Level Advanced

This origami model is designed using several interlocked rectangles. To create a successful card it is very important that you half-cut all the lines properly; if not, you may experience some problems when you begin to fold. Keep in mind that you need to guide each of the folds, forming them a little at a time—this will help you to achieve the best results. (*See template on page 97.*)

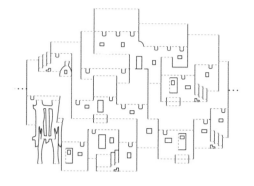

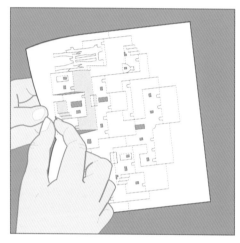

1 Looking at the printed side of the card, push back the valley folds at the base of the town—not to the end of the fold lines, but just enough to mark the folds. Extra attention is needed when folding the flights of steps as they can be quite fiddly.

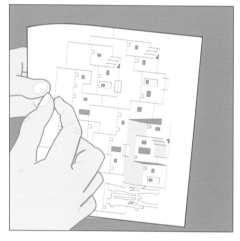

2 Turn the card around, and work in the same way on the valley lines on the roofs of the buildings, pushing back enough to mark the folds.

3 Now fold the central gutter line upward slightly, using your thumbs and index fingers, with the rest of your fingers below the paper.

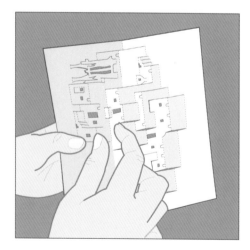

4 Turning the card as much as necessary, push back the valley lines on the middle of the card to work on the buildings, little steps, etc. If you have successfully half-cut the mountain lines, you will notice that they fold with very little assistance.

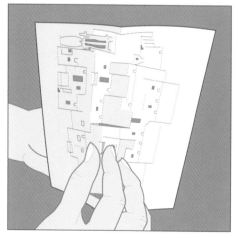

5 Next, work on the single steps by carefully pinching them. Turn the template over. With one hand holding the base of the model, use your other hand to push from the back of the card toward you. Once again, be careful with the small steps.

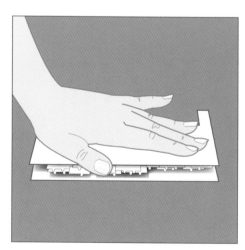

6 Once all the folds are formed, place the card on a flat surface, and press down firmly. Lastly, open up the card and push the doors slightly inward to the rooms.

U.S. Capitol The Model

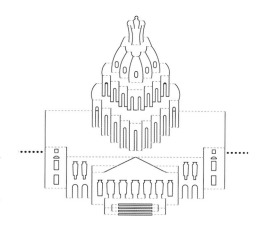

  Origami Architect María Victoria Garrido Bianchini

★★★ **Difficulty Level** Advanced

This emblematic building is recognized by its beautiful dome which stands over the Rotunda. It is the dome that makes this origamic model particularly impressive, too. It may look as though it is a difficult area to fold, but if you form the half-cuts correctly, you will find it almost folds itself. (*See template on page 99.*)

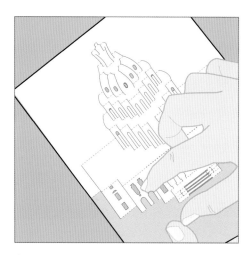

1 Looking at the printed side of the card, push back the valley folds on the base of the building and the roof. Now fold the gutter slightly—just enough to mark the fold. Continue to push all the valley folds in a gradual, smooth progression.

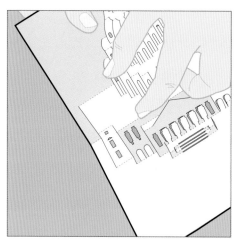

2 Holding the card by the roof of the building, push along the mountain lines to mark the folds. Be patient: you have to work continually and slowly on all folds.

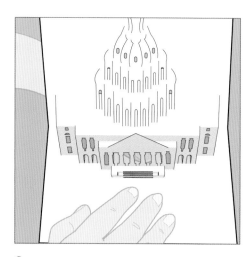

3 Turn the card over, so that you are looking at the unprinted side. With one hand on the steps, use your other hand to push from the back. Now use a bamboo skewer to push back the middle steps. Once the steps are formed, fold the valley lines to the end at the base of the building.

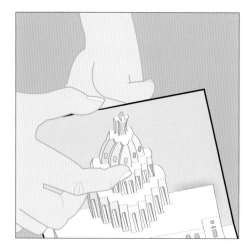

4 Turn the card over again, so that you are now looking at the printed side of the paper. Turn your attention to the dome. Work the valley folds, pushing backward very slowly and working on all the folds at the same time.

5 With one hand steadying the base of the card, use your other hand to push the building toward your left, thereby making the various steps on the dome. Be very careful: if you have half-cut properly, it will fold easily.

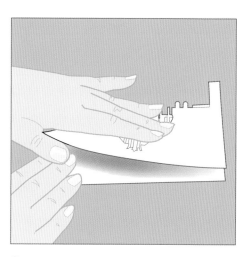

6 Now, with both hands, slowly close the card along the center, ensuring that all folds are correct. Once you are sure that all the folds are in the correct positions, place the card on a flat surface, and press down firmly. Open up to display your model.

U.S. Capitol Built *1793–1824* CE

Architects **William Thornton, Stephen Hallet, Benjamin Henry Latrobe, Charles Bulfinch, Thomas U. Walter, and August Schoenborn**

Location Washington DC, U.S.A.

Style Neoclassic

Purpose Seat of U.S. Congress

Materials Sandstone, brick, stucco, marble, wood, copper, and cast iron

Area 175,170 sq ft (16,258 sq m)

Features 540 rooms, 850 doors, 658 windows and 365 steps (west front)

Decoration Bronze doors, sculpture, statues

Cost to build $133 million

The U.S. Capitol sits on Capitol Hill, about a mile southeast of the White House in Washington, DC. This emblematic building is recognized by its beautiful dome, which stands over the graciously proportioned Rotunda. The Capitol's nineteenth-century neoclassic architecture combines function with aesthetics. The building's site was chosen by President George Washington's city planner, Pierre Charles l'Enfant, with Washington himself laying the first sandstone cornerstone in 1793. The building was designed by William Thornton (1759–1828) and inspired by some of the great domed buildings of ancient and medieval Europe, such as the dome of the Roman Pantheon and the Renaissance domes of St. Peter's Basilica in Rome and the Duomo in Florence.

The building is divided into two wings. Originally these were connected by a wooden passageway; however, after the building was partially burned by British troops in 1814 it was reconstructed by Benjamin Henry Latrobe (1764–1820) and Charles Bulfinch (1763–1844). The new building included a massive copper-and-wood dome, which covered the celebrated Rotunda and provided a new link between the two wings.

The wings were designed as homes for the two houses of Congress—the Senate in the North Wing (completed 1800) and the House of Representatives in the South Wing (completed 1811). By the end of the U.S. Civil War in 1865, under the guidance of the army engineer Montgomery Meigs (1816–1892), the massive new wings and dome—designed by Thomas U. Walter (1804–1887) and August Schoenborn (approx. 1827–1902)—had taken shape. Fresco painter Constantino Brumidi (1805–1880) spent the next quarter of a century decorating the interior.

The present dome was designed by Thomas U. Walter in 1854, as part of an expansion to accommodate the increased number of people in the Senate and the House of Representatives. The cast-iron, fireproof double dome—three times the height of its predecessor—was completed in 1866. It was constructed using 84,450 tons (4,041 tonnes) of iron. The Rotunda remains underneath, a circular ceremonial space and art gallery, with the famous 19-foot (5.8-m) Statue of Freedom on the pinnacle of the dome above it.

Number of visitors per year
♙♙ = up to 1 million

Number of years to build
Ť = 1 year

Height of the structure

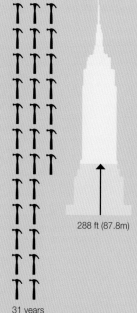

4 million visitors

31 years

288 ft (87.8m)

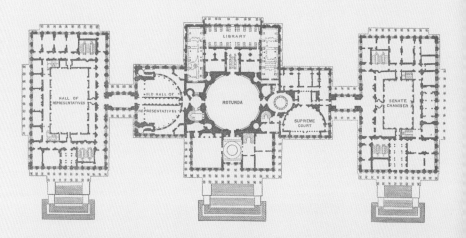

Floor plan of the U.S. Capitol, showing the central Rotunda for which it is so well known. A series of underground tunnels link the main building with the surrounding Congressional office buildings, and there is even a private underground railway system.

Rialto Bridge
Built *1588–1591* CE

Architect **Antonio da Ponte**

The Rialto Bridge is one of the most elegant and recognizable bridges in the world, spanning the Grand Canal in Venice in a single arch tall enough to allow gondolas to pass underneath. The Venetians replaced many failing wooden bridges with stone ones during the fifteenth and sixteenth centuries, and the new bridges needed to be taller to make room for the raised cabins that were becoming popular on the gondolas of the nobility. The wooden Rialto Bridge was in a poor state by the early 1500s, but the Venetian government ignored complaints until 1588. When the government agreed to its reconstruction, it commissioned Antonio da Ponte (1512–c.1595)—a master builder who had worked on other Venetian civic projects—to replace it. He chose to build with Istrian stone, a material also used for other Venetian landmarks such as the Ponte dei Sospiri (Bridge of Sighs) and Palazzo Ducale (Doge's Palace). He supported the stone with thousands of extra wooden pilings, which were driven into the canal bed to bear the weight of the stone structure.

On either side of the columns and pediments of the crowning central portico, there are two covered arcades that eventually join the portico at a gentle gradient. Each arcade has six rounded arches comprising a broad central promenade and a narrow corridor along each balustrade, featuring cramped shops with lead-covered roofs. It was a close copy, in this respect, of the wooden bridge that had preceded it.

Many Venetians doubted the bridge could support the weight of the main portico, but it has survived to this day by resting on the same 12,000 wooden pilings that Antonio da Ponte originally drove into the banks. For decoration, and for divine support, Ponte placed a number of religious statues at the entrances to the bridge: St. Mark and St. Theodore are on one end and the Annunciation is depicted at the other end.

Location Venice, Italy

Style Venetian, Renaissance

Purpose Footbridge

Materials Istrian stone, wood, and lead

Area 1,890 sq ft (173 sq m)

Cost to build 250 ducats

Wooden pilings 12,000

Features 3 walkways and 24 shops

Number of visitors per year
!! = up to 1 million

12 million visitors

Number of years to build
T = 1 year

3 years

Height of the structure

23.9 ft (7.3m)

The side elevation of the Rialto Bridge. The interior of this stone-covered bridge has a double row of stone arches that provide much of the structure's strength. The bridge is now lit front and back.

Rialto Bridge The Model

Origami Architect María Victoria Garrido Bianchini

Difficulty Level Intermediate

Here you can re-create one of the most romantic bridges in the world. Start by cutting out the windows and doors of the small shops, then turn your attention to lines at the roof of the bridge and the two flights of steps. The cutting process is fairly simple, but folding the steps is not so easy. Just take your time and form each fold gradually, a little at a time. (*See template on page 101.*)

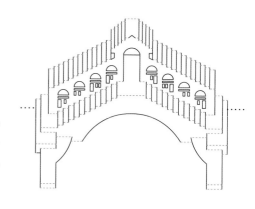

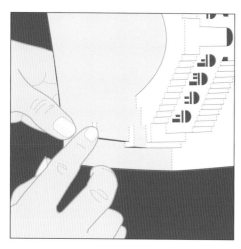

1 Looking at the printed side of the paper, push back the valley line at the base of the bridge—just enough to mark the fold.

2 Now fold the central gutter line upward a little.

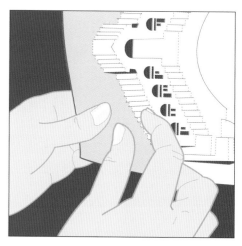

3 Turn the card around, and push back the valley folds on the roof of the bridge. Also gently work the valley lines on the two extremes of the bridge to mark the folds.

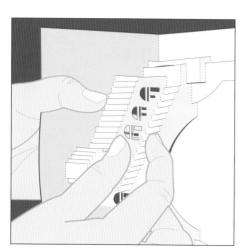

4 With one hand, hold the card near to the windows area. With your other hand, take hold of the bridge and push it back to create the valley folds on the steps. You will find that the mountain folds follow naturally.

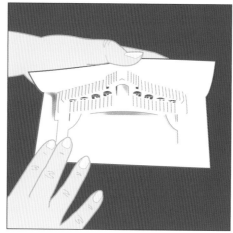

5 Turn the card over, so that you are looking at the unprinted side. Holding the card at the base of the bridge with one hand, use your other hand to push from the back of the card toward you. Be particularly careful when folding the base of the building.

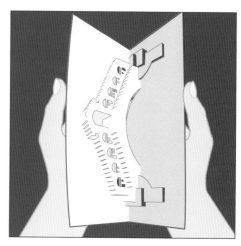

6 Slowly close the card along the center, ensuring that all folds are correct. Once you are sure that all the folds are in the correct position, place the card on a flat surface, and press down firmly. Open up to display your model.

Empire State Building The Model

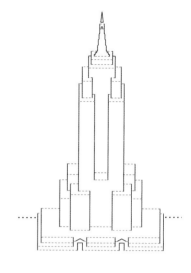

▲ **Origami Architect** Joyce Aysta

★★★ **Difficulty Level** Advanced

This design with its many closely spaced folds may be difficult. Using a bamboo skewer, as described on page 9 under folding tips, makes this model easier—especially at the base. (*See template on page 103.*)

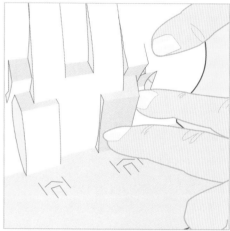

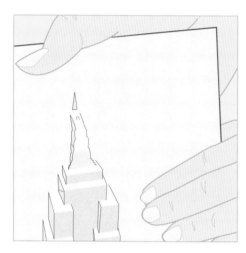

1 Begin folding this template from the top. As the stand-offs are only ⅛" (3mm) deep, folding is a little more difficult. Holding the card from the top, gently push out the tower.

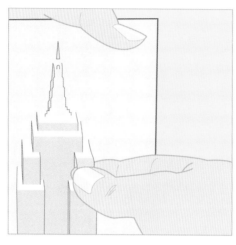

2 Carefully work your way down the spires, folding the stand-offs one at a time. When you reach the midpoint, work from both the right and the left.

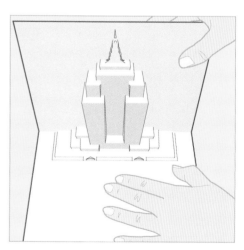

3 Gently fold the gutter line and the side towers down to where they meet the base platform.

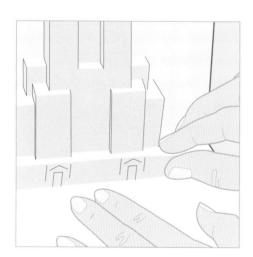

4 Now for the hard part. Holding the card at the bottom, fold the base valley line (all three lengths of it), then the mountain line three folds up with the tops of the doors.

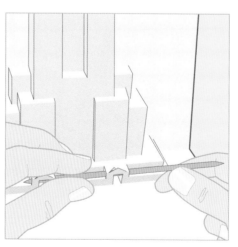

5 Finally, push the three sets of two folds remaining from the front through to the back to create the three stand-offs near the base. You may wish to use a bamboo skewer to help form the correct shapes.

6 With both hands, slowly close the card along the gutter fold, ensuring that all folds are correct. Once you are sure that they are in the right position, place the card on a flat surface and press firmly. Open up to display your model.

Empire State Building Built *1930–1931 c.*

Architect **William Lamb of Shreve,**

Lamb & Harmon Associates

The Empire State Building is one of the most distinctive buildings in New York City and arguably the most famous skyscraper in the world. Its construction was the result of a contest between John J. Raskob and Walter Chrysler, whose rival Chrysler Building was completed in 1930, to build the tallest building. Architect William Lamb produced the first blueprints for the steel-frame design in just two weeks. It was built during the Great Depression on the site of the old Waldorf-Astoria hotel and became the first skyscraper to exceed one hundred floors. At 1,250 feet (381m), it was the tallest building in the world until 1972.

The building has Indiana limestone cladding and aluminum spandrel panels, with two-story corridors around the elevator core. It now houses 1,000 businesses and 20,000 employees, serviced by 7 banks. After the World Trade Center was destroyed in 2001, the Empire State Building became New York's tallest building once again.

While the Empire State Building lacks the distinctive zigzag decoration of Art Deco, its form does reflect the geometric shapes that characterize the style—especially in the shape of the tower. It combines this spirit of Art Deco with restrained gray classical façades and Modernist stainless-steel canopies. The façade is enhanced by the use of floodlights on the upper part of the building, which were installed in 1964. The lights illuminate three tiers of the façade and change color for notable occasions such as St. Patrick's Day, Independence Day, and other special events.

The pinnacle of the building is its most famous and recognizable feature—it houses observation decks on the 86th and 102nd floors. The spire itself was originally designed to be a mooring mast for dirigible airships, but this proved impractical and it was closed early in the life of the building. In place of the mooring mast, a large telecommunications tower was added in 1954.

 Location New York City, U.S.A.

 Style Art Deco

 Purpose Office building

 Materials Steel, Indiana limestone, aluminum, brick, glass, Rosa Famosa, and Estrallante marble

 Area 79,288 sq ft (7,240 sq m)

 Features 1,000 companies, 6,500 windows, 1,860 steps, 67 elevators, and 14 escalators

 Decoration Spandrel paneling

 Cost to build $27,718,000 (building), $40,948,900 (building and land)

Number of visitors to observatories per year
** = up to 1 million

Number of years to build
T = 1 year

Height of the structure

3.8 million visitors

1 year

1,250 ft (381m)

The pinnacle of the Empire State Building, originally designed to facilitate disembarking from passenger balloons, remains one of its most distinctive features. It is now covered with broadcast antennas, and has a lightning rod at the topmost point.

St. Peter's Basilica Built *1506–1626* CE

Architects **Donato Bramante** (1505)**, Raphael Sanzio** (1513)**, Michelangelo** (1563)**, and Carlo Maderno** (1626)

St. Peter's Basilica is the heart of the Roman Catholic Church, the Pope's own cathedral at the center of the Vatican City. It was the brainchild of the warrior-pope Julius II, who wanted to rebuild the dilapidated old St. Peter's on a grander scale. By 1505, his architect Donato Bramante (1444–1514) had designed a massive Greek-cross plan with a dome, modeled on the Pantheon in Rome. Julius II laid the foundation stone in 1506, but he died in 1513; he was never able to see the finished building. The artist Raphael Sanzio (1483–1520) introduced a new design with a nave and a series of chapels along the sides, but it was Michelangelo (1475–1564) who modified, simplified, and strengthened Bramante's Greek-cross plan. He eliminated the smaller cruciform units, corner towers, and ambulatories by the apses, and widened the four slender piers.

The most dramatic feature of the basilica today is the massive oval dome—the tallest in the world—with sixteen stone ribs and sixteen pairs of Corinthian columns. There is still controversy about why the dome design was changed to an oval shape. However, most scholars agree that it was not only to give the appearance of stretching up toward the heavens, but also to decrease the lateral thrust and to force weight onto the drum.

The building was completed by Carlo Maderno (1556–1629) in 1626. His most obvious contribution is the façade, made of travertine stone and dominated by giant Corinthian columns holding up a large pediment. The design of the façade was lengthened to include two towers at either end, which were kept small because the ground beneath was considered too weak to bear their weight. Critics have been harsh about the façade, which obscures the view of the dome, calling it one of the least satisfactory aspects of the overall design.

Location Rome, Italy

Style High Renaissance, Baroque

Purpose Roman Catholic basilica

Materials Travertine, brick, stucco, marble, gilt, and bronze

Area 260,776 sq ft (24,224 sq m)

Cost to build 46,800,052 ducats

Capacity 60,000 people

Features 3 domes, Corinthian columns, portals, 2 transepts, 1 nave, 1 vestibule, piers, 44 statues, 24 altars, and tombs

Number of visitors per year
‼ = up to 1 million

‼ ‼ ‼
‼

4 million visitors

Number of years to build
⏰ = up to 20 years

⏰ ⏰
⏰ ⏰
⏰ ⏰

120 years

Height of the structure

149.4 ft (45.5m)

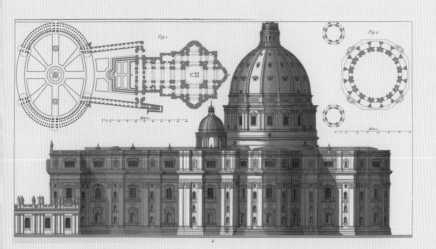

An engraving of St. Peter's Basilica. The floorplan above left shows St. Peter's Square leading up to the basilica; the floorplan above right is of Michelangelo's famous dome.

St. Peter's Basilica The Model

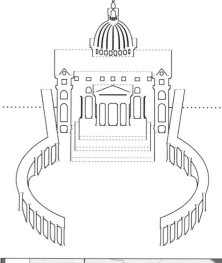

 Origami Architect Joyce Aysta

 Difficulty Level Advanced

This design is more difficult to cut than many of the others because of the small shapes. There are eleven figures on the front edge of the roof. They are too small and complex to be cut by hand at this scale, however, so I have not included them. (*See template on page 105.*)

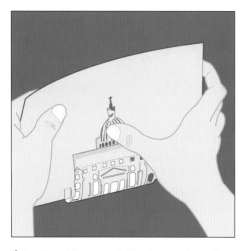

1 Looking at the printed side of the card, gently push the dome out.

2 Turn the card over to the unprinted side. Slowly work your way toward the central gutter fold, creasing the roof structure valley folds and mountain folds, the valley folds at the back of the two colonnades, and finally the gutter fold itself.

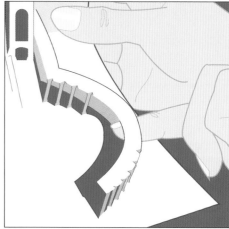

3 Turn the card 180 degrees to work from the bottom of the card. Gently pull out the two colonnades (they will fold as a unit). Ensure that you pull them up all the way, so that the tops and bottoms of the columns crease fully.

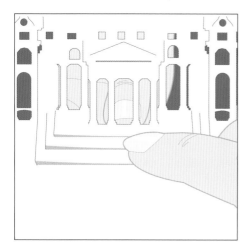

4 Now, holding the card at the base, start working the valley fold at the foot of the steps. Progress up the steps, one fold at a time, gathering them in your hand accordion-fashion.

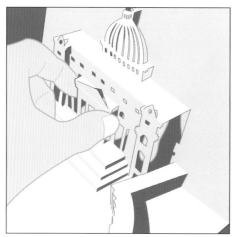

5 Once you have successfully completed the steps, turn your attention to the portico, gently pushing it outward.

6 Gently close the card, ensuring that the colonnades come completely forward and the cornices on the sides don't catch on each other. Place the card on a flat surface, and press down firmly. Open up to display the model.

Sagrada Família The Model

  Origami Architect Ingrid Siliakus

★★★ **Difficulty Level** Advanced

An origamic architecture card based on this template was exhibited in the Sagrada Família in 2004. It is an advanced model that requires many delicate cuts and folds, so don't attempt it before mastering some of the earlier models. The finished result is beautiful, though, so it is well worth the perseverance. (*See template on page 107.*)

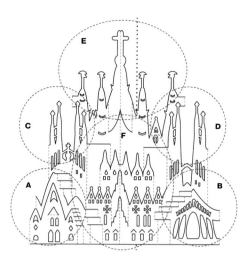

1 Divide the card into regions (see diagram, top right), and work your way through, folding each one in turn. Start with **Region A**, supporting the lower-left part with your left hand. With your right hand, carefully tilt this region into shape toward your left hand, until it is almost folded entirely. Do the same for **Region B**.

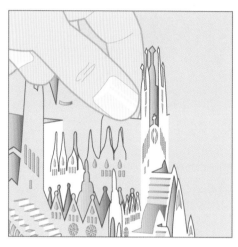

2 Fold **C** and **D**, using the tips of your index fingers and thumbs to support the back and front. While working on these individual regions, the other parts of the card automatically fold in and out. Support these parts if they start to fold in the wrong direction.

3 Region E is the hardest to fold. Place your middle fingers and thumbs at the back and front on both sides of the towers next to the biggest tower. Fold the valley and mountain folds by pushing the part between your fingers and thumbs together. Use your thumbnail in the valley folds to press them out at the back of the card.

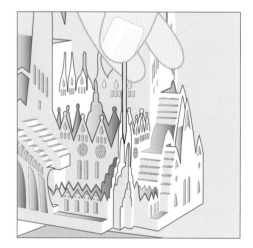

4 For **Region F**, place your bamboo skewer behind the mountain folds. Push the folds to the front with the skewer while squeezing them at the same time, keeping your fingers on both sides of the folds. Now use the length of the skewer to push back some of the valley folds in this region.

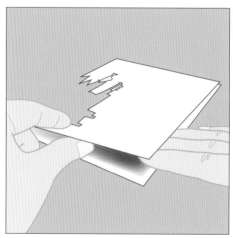

5 Place the card on its side, and hold the upper part with one hand. With your other hand, squeeze together the folds that you can get hold of. Gently squeeze them bit by bit, and slowly close the card entirely. Open up to display your model.

Sagrada Família Built *1882–due approx. 2026* CE

Architects **Antonio Gaudí** (1883) **and Francisco de Villar** (1882)
Architects since 1940 **Francesc Quintana** (1944)**, Isidre Puig Boada** (1950)**, Lluis Bonet i Gari** (1954)**, and Francesc Cardoner** (1983)

Location Barcelona, Spain

Style Expressionist, neo-Gothic, Art Nouveau

Purpose Catholic temple

Materials Limestone, mosaic tiles

Area 58,115 sq ft (5,400 sq m)

Decoration stone carvings

Features 12 bell towers, 8 spires, 6 domes, 5 naves, and 7 chapels

Cost to build $3.2 million (cost at 1995)

The Sagrada Família (Holy Family) is a Catholic basilica partially built by Antonio Gaudí. In 1875, neo-Gothic plans had been drawn up under Francisco de Villar and construction began in 1882. De Villar resigned in 1883, however, and Gaudí took over. He worked on the project until his death in 1926. Partly due to funding, just the east façade, one tower and its bell towers, one chapel, and the crypt had been finished at his death. However, Gaudí had designed many fluid sculptures and serpentine curves that made his building resemble a living organism or petrified forest.

Gaudí had planned eighteen mosaic-decorated spires of different heights, representing Christ, the Virgin, the four evangelists, and the twelve apostles. To date, there are eight spires rising from a square base to become tubes, spirals, and finials. Six domes represent Christ, the Virgin, and the evangelists as well. There are three entrance façades, each with four bell towers: east (the Nativity), finished by Gaudí; west (the Passion), started in 1954 by the controversial sculptor Josep Maria Subirachs, now complete; and south (the Glory), which remains unfinished at present.

The floor plan is like a Latin cross, with three transepts and five naves. Around the apse are seven chapels, an ambulatory, and a presbytery. Columns are often conical and striated, and they lean, branch, and change form as they rise. Capitals are ellipsoid, decorated with symbols.

Construction slowed after Gaudí's death due to funding and destruction of his models during the Spanish Civil War (1936). Building did not resume until the mid-1950s (west façade). To date, two façades, eight towers and their bell towers, vaults to the central nave and transepts, and the apse are largely finished. Completion is planned for 2026, the centenary of Gaudí's death.

Number of visitors per year
‼ = up to 1 million

2 million visitors

Number of years to build
① = up to 20 years

① ①
① ①
① ①
① ①

144 years (expected)

Eventual height of the structure

558 ft (170m)

A pen-and-ink sketch by Gaudí showing the Nativity façade, dedicated to the birth of Christ. This was the first part of the Sagrada Família to be completed and remains true to his original design.

Hagia Sophia Built *532–537* CE

Architects **Isidore of Miletus, Anthemius of Tralles**

The Hagia Sophia (formerly the Church of the Holy Wisdom), with its complex combinations of domes and mosaics, is among the greatest examples of Byzantine architecture. It has inspired the look of churches and mosques across the Eastern Orthodox, Roman Catholic, and Muslim worlds. Although originally built as a church, it is now one of the most famous Islamic buildings in existence. Other churches stood on the same site, but when one of these was destroyed in 532 CE, Emperor Justinian I commissioned the original Hagia Sophia, which was designed by the mathematicians Isidore and Anthemius.

The architects supported the basilica's famous central dome with four piers that have buttressed arches linked by pendentives, the stone supports that fit a circular dome over a four-sided building. Light flooding in from the windows makes the dome appear to float above the rest of the building. Flanking semidomes at the ends of the nave create an oblong interior that was unprecedented when it was first built. Unfortunately, the dome kept collapsing, most recently in 1346, and it is now slightly elliptical. It now has extra support from giant buttresses outside the building, built by the Ottomans in the fifteenth century.

When the Ottoman Mehmet II seized Constantinople (present-day Instanbul) in 1453, he converted the building into a mosque. A mihrab (prayer niche), minbar (pulpit), and minarets were added. The figurative Byzantine imagery was plastered over because Islamic codes forbade representations of the human figure. The minarets—one in red brick and three in white marble—are the most recognizable Islamic features of the building.

Improvements continued to the building throughout the eighteenth and nineteenth centuries, notably in 1849 when the minarets were made more congruous. In 1935, Kemal Atatürk, father of the new Turkish Republic, secularized the mosque and converted it into the Ayasofya Museum.

Location Istanbul, Turkey

Style Byzantine, Ottoman

Purpose Basilica (original), mosque, and museum

Materials Brick masonry, stucco, marble, and glass

Area 56,580 sq ft (5,250 sq m)

Features 230 windows, 9 doors, and 4 piers

Decoration Polychrome marble, gold mosaics, icons, seraphims (on pendentives), mihrab, and minbar

Cost to build 20,000 lb gold

Number of visitors per year = up to 1 million	Number of years to build = 1 year	Height of the structure
2 million visitors	5 years	182 ft (55.5m)

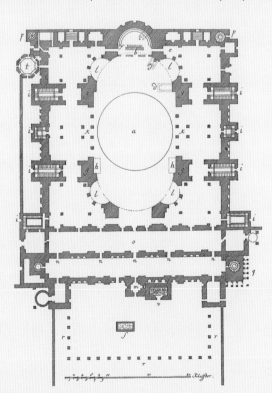

Floor plan of Hagia Sophia showing the position of the great central dome. The dome is supported by four great arches made of stone, which in turn rest on a series of smaller semidomes.

Hagia Sophia The Model

Origami Architect Ingrid Siliakus

Difficulty Level Advanced

This is an extensive project. The windows, especially at the bottom of the template, are in close proximity to one another, so you must take care not to break the small intersecting parts. Use a sharp blade in your craft knife. If it proves too difficult, you can create larger windows instead by cutting out the intersections between the windows as well as the actual windows. (*See template on page 109.*)

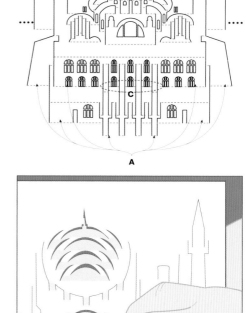

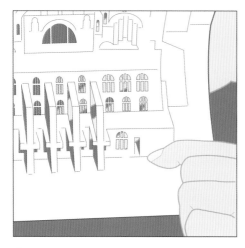

1 Fold in the central gutter line, left and right, while pushing the model forward with one hand from the back. Concentrate on pushing forward the fold lines located in **Region A**. Put your nails into the valley folds, while pushing forward with your other hand from the back.

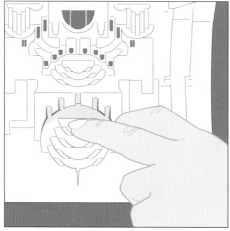

2 Turn the template 180 degrees and do the same for the fold lines located in **Region B**. Repeat step 1 a few times on both **A** and **B**, until the fold lines are pressed in by approximately a quarter.

3 Rotate the template back 180 degrees. Push in the valley folds on the roof, using your nails on the front while pushing with one hand from the back. It helps to put the thumb and index finger of your hand on the back of the card on either side of the fold line, and squeeze together.

4 Turn over the template, so that you are looking at the printed side, and do the same to the mountain folds. At this stage, you will notice that, on both the back and front of the card, some areas have a tendency to turn inward or come to the front. Focus on these areas next.

5 Turn the card over. Insert a skewer behind the mountain folds, beginning at the pillars in **Region C**. Tilt these mountain folds forward and up to bring them into shape. Do the same to all other mountain folds. Work your way up, first on the smaller folds of the roof, then on the longer fold lines.

6 Hold the card steady while tilting the fold lines forward and up with the skewer. To make the shape of the two towers, tilt the fold lines forward and up individually while holding either side of the tower. Continue with all the folds until the card can be closed. Open up to display your model.

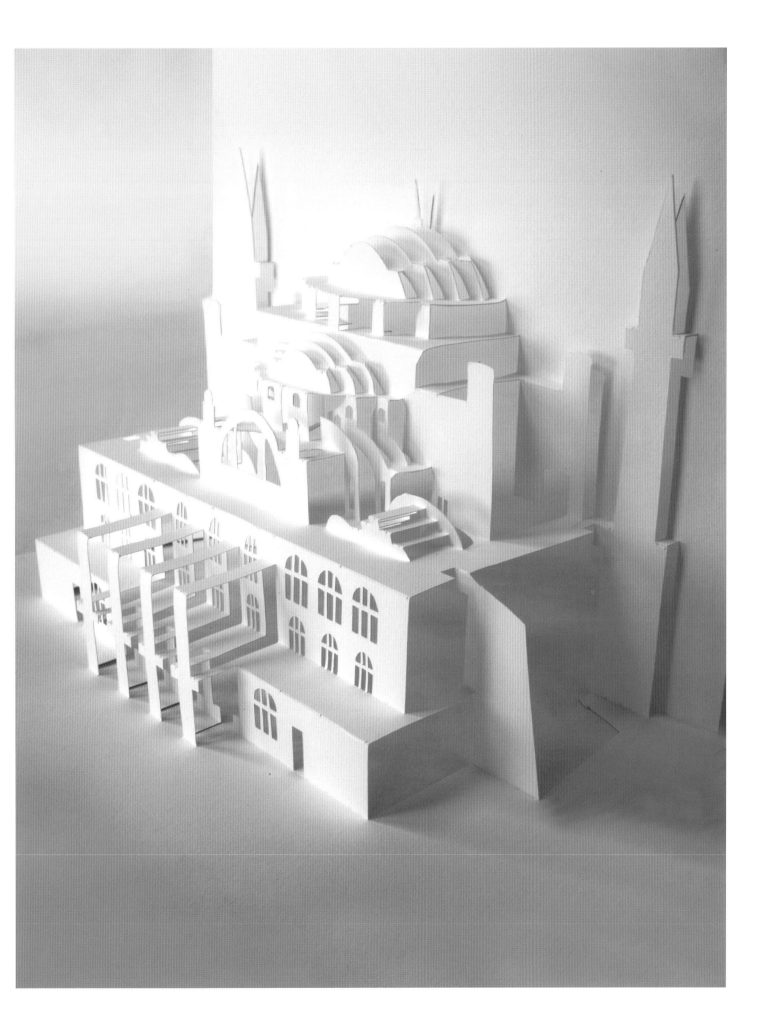

Resources

A.C. Moore
Corporate Office
130 A.C. Moore Drive,
Berlin, NJ 08009
1-888-ACMOORE OPTION-2
www.acmoore.com
• Arts and crafts suppliers with stores across America.
See website for store locations.

Dick Blick
P.O. Box 1267
Galesburg, IL 61402-1267
1-800-828-4548
www.dickblick.com
• Art materials suppliers. Products can be ordered
online or purchased instore. See website for store
locations.

Graphic Products Corporation
455 Maple Ave.
Carpenterville, IL 60110
1-847-836-9600
www.gpcpapers.com
• Supplier of graphic arts products. Products are
available to order online and at various stores
across America. See website for store locations.

Hiromi Paper International
2525 Michigan Ave., Unit G-9
Santa Monica, CA 90404
1-866-479-2744
www.hiromipaper.com
• Supplier of Japanese paper. Products are available
to order online. See website for details.

Jo-Ann
Corporate Office
5555 Darrow Rd.
Hudson, OH 44236
1-888-739-4120
www.joann.com
• Supplier of fabric and craft products. Order online
or see website for store locations.

Kelly Paper
Corporate Office
288 Brea Canyon Rd.
City of Industry, CA 91789
1-800-675-3559
www.kellypaper.com
• A wholesale paper supplier. Products can be
ordered online or purchased instore. See website
for store locations.

Legion Paper
11 Madison Ave.
New York, NY 10010
1-800-278-4478
(International): (212) 683-6990
www.legionpaper.com
• Supplier of fine art paper. Order online or see
website for store locations.

Michaels Stores, Inc.
8000 Bent Branch Dr.
Irving, TX 75063
1-800-642-4235
www.michaels.com
• Arts and crafts suppliers with stores across America.
Products can be viewed online, but are only available
for purchase instore. See website for store locations.

Mister Art
913 Willard St.
Houston, TX 77006
1-800-721-3015
www.misterart.com
• Online discount arts and crafts store.

Pearl
1033 E. Oakland Park Blvd.
Fort Lauderdale,
FL 33334
1-800-451-7327
www.pearlpaint.com
• Suppliers of art and craft materials. Purchase online
or see website for store locations.

For further advice and product information, please
contact the authors:

Ingrid Siliakus
E: paperartnl@yahoo.com
http://ingrid-siliakus.exto.org

Joyce Aysta
Live Your Dream Designs
323-226-0274
E: orders@liveyourdreamdesigns.com
www.liveyourdreamdesigns.com

María Victoria Garrido Bianchini
E: marivi_2@yahoo.com
www.geocities.com/marivi_2/index.html

Golden Gate Bridge (See instructions on page 10.)

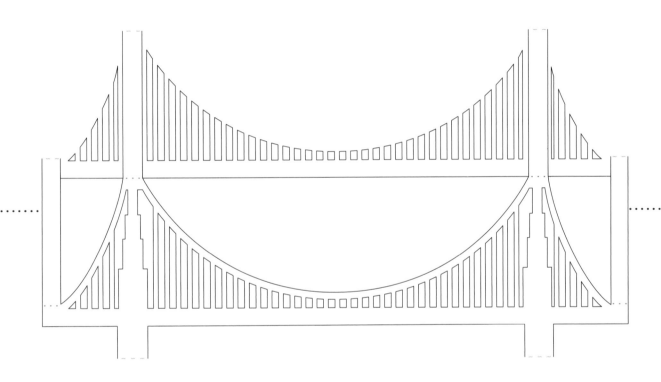

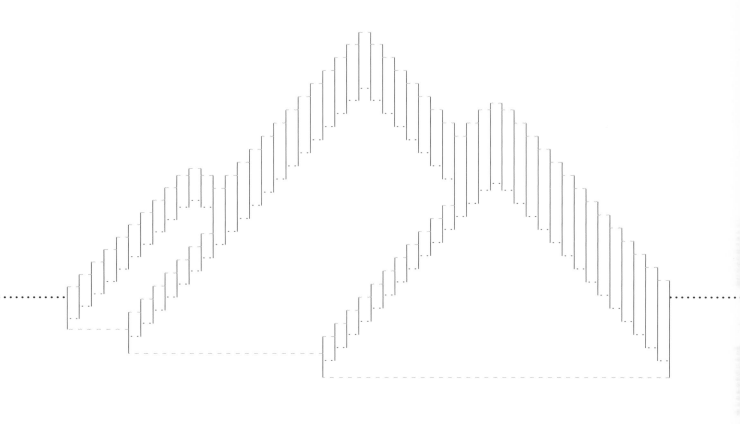

Chichén Itzá (See instructions on page 20.)

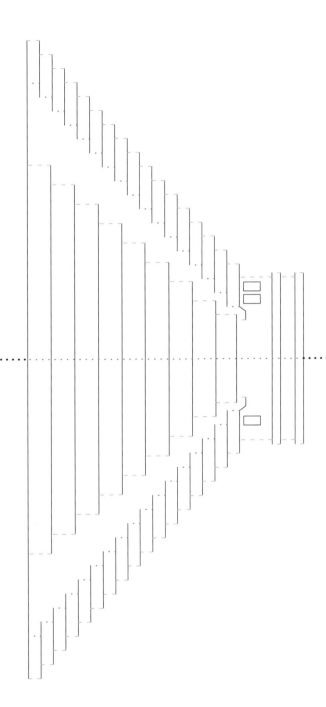

Seagram Building / Eiffel Tower (See instructions on pages 22 and 26.)

Parthenon (See instructions on page 28.)

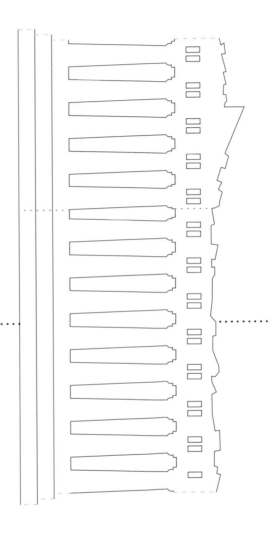

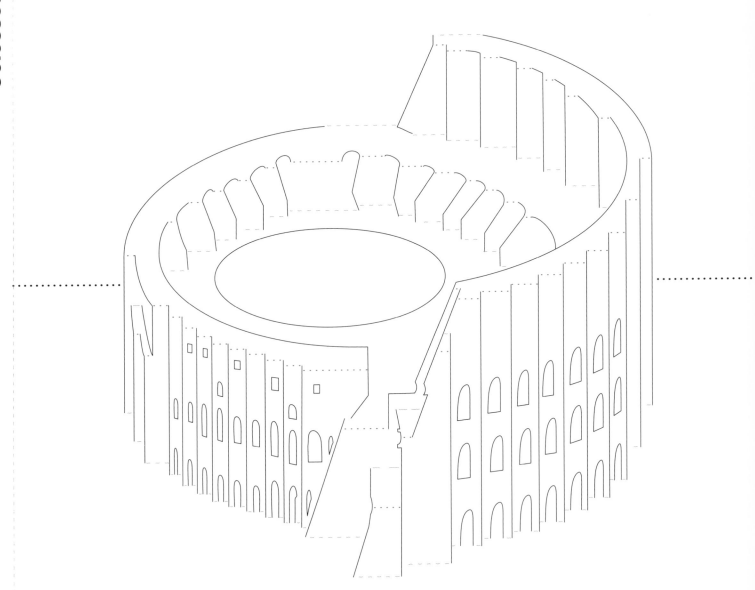

Golden Pavilion (See instructions on page 34.)

White House A (See instructions on page 40.)

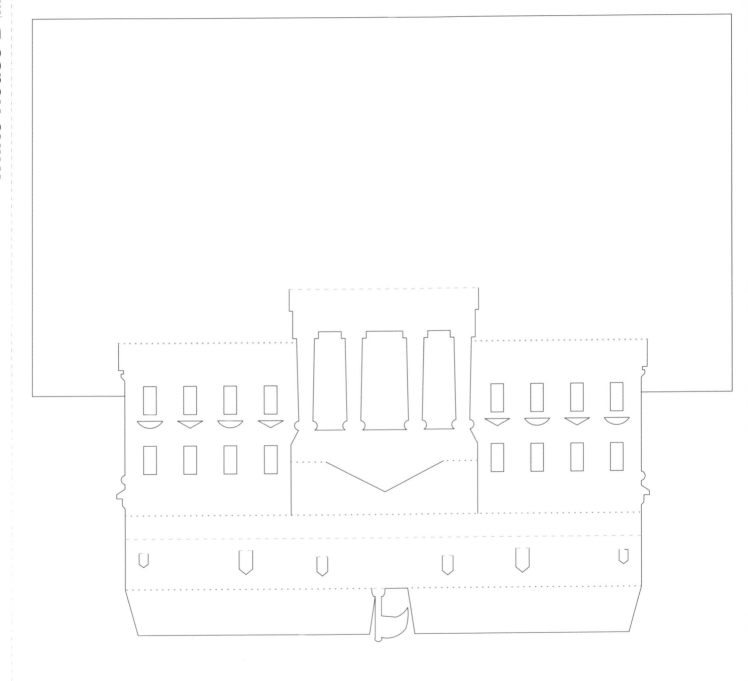

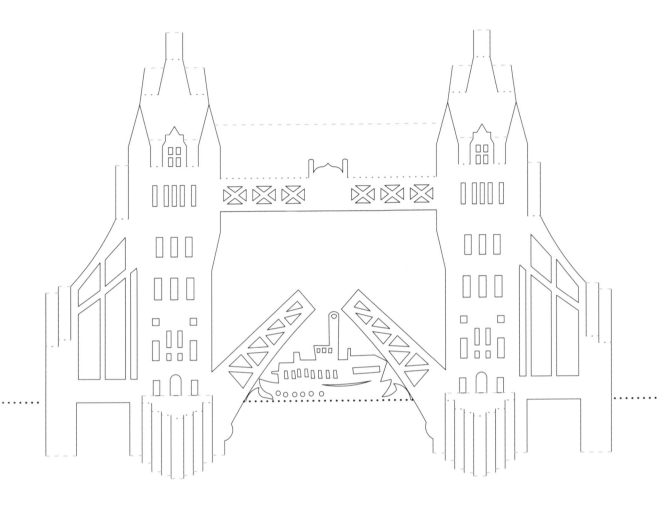

Taos Pueblo
(See instructions on page 50.)

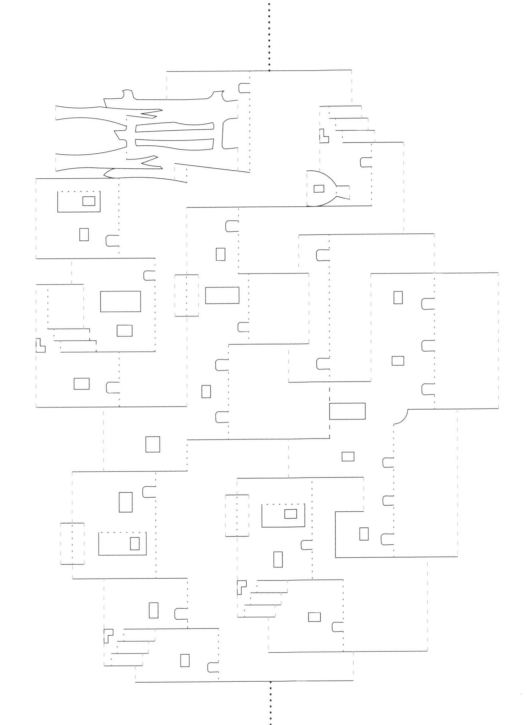

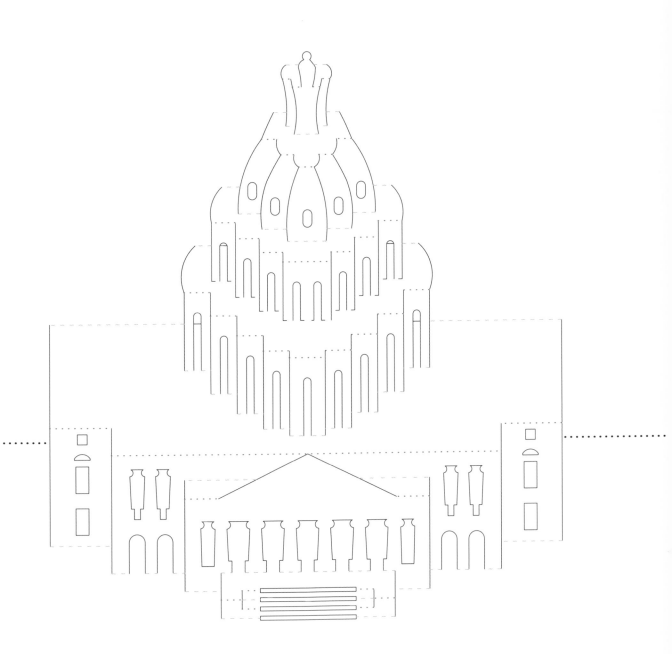

Rialto Bridge (See instructions on page 56.)

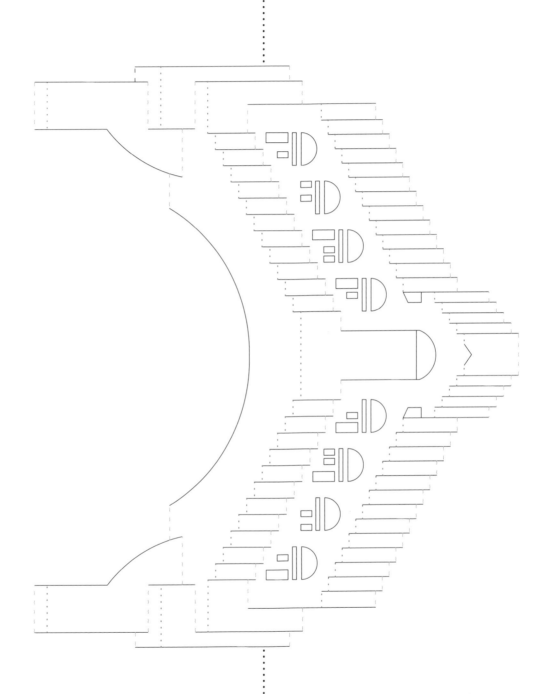

Empire State Building (See instructions on page 58.)

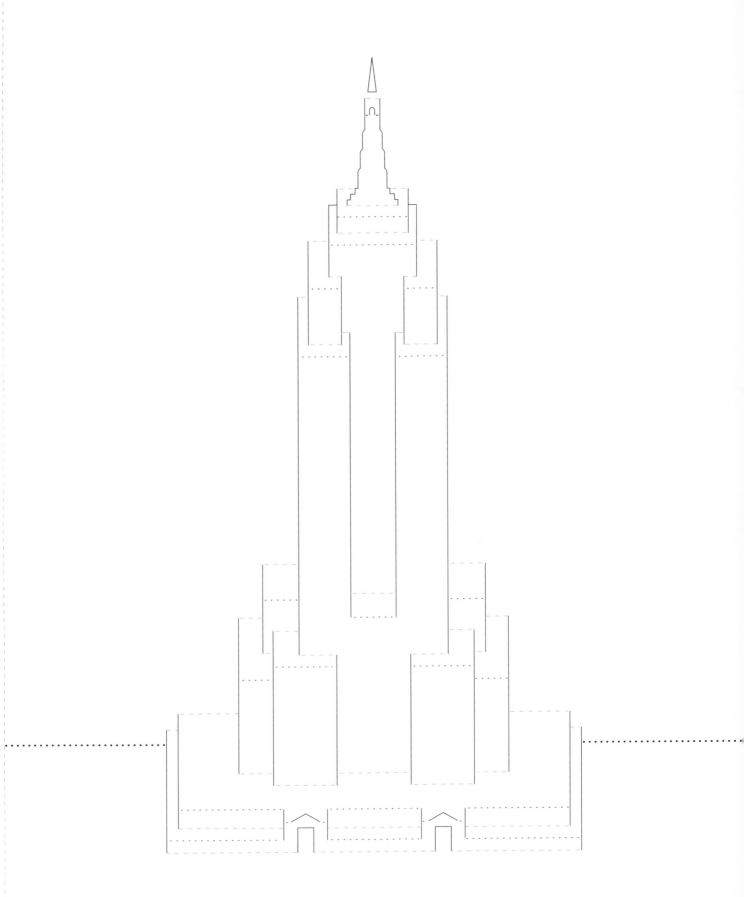

St Peter's Basilica (See instructions on page 62.)

Hagia Sophia (See instructions on page 68.)